PRESSURE PROOF YOUR RIDING

Mental Training Techniques
Gain Confidence and Get Motivated So You (and Your Horse) Achieve Peak Performance

DANIEL STEWART

TRAFALGAR SQUARE
North Pomfret, Vermont

First published in 2013 by
Trafalgar Square Books
North Pomfret, Vermont 05053

Printed in China

Disclaimer of Liability
The author and publisher shall have neither liability nor responsibility to any person or entity with respect to any loss or damage caused or alleged to be caused directly or indirectly by the information contained in this book. While the book is as accurate as the author can make it, there may be errors, omissions, and inaccuracies.

Trafalgar Square Books encourages the use of approved safety helmets in all equestrian sports and activities.

The author and publisher have made every effort to obtain a release from photographers whose images appear in this book. In some cases, however, the photographers were not known or could not be contacted. Should additional photographers be identified, they will be credited in future editions of this book.

Library of Congress Cataloging-in-Publication Data

Stewart, Daniel.
  Pressure proof your riding : gain confidence and get motivated so you (and your horse) achieve peak performance / Daniel Stewart.
    pages cm
    Includes index.
  ISBN 978-1-57076-541-4 (pbk.)
  1. Horsemanship. 2. Horsemanship--Psychological aspects. I. Title.
  SF309.S834 2013
  798.2--dc23
                          2013009673

Cartoons by Erin Smith
Photographs by: Efecreata Photography/shutterstock.com (p. 2); Samantha Hunt-Garbarino (p. 6); Mark Walter Lehner (pp. 10, 224); James Schuessler (pp. 23, 42, 95, 244, 249); Michael Ruhs (pp. 35, 65, 70, 190, 231, 240); D'Arlene Beard Photography (pp. 17, 45, 47, 57, 90, 98, 136, 146, 234); Norman Chan/shutterstock.com (p. 26); Josh Walker for Shannon Brinkman Photo (p. 38); Kelsey Stevens (p. 74, 200); Christopher Halloran/shutterstock.com (p. 102); Mike McNally (p. 149); Denise Polacek (pp. 142, 251); Emily Shoemake (p. 161); Efecreata Photography/shutterstock.com (p. 168); Stephanie Walty (p. 172); John Oren (p. 242); Terry Abrams (p. 243); Leslie Patterson (p. 246); Susan Jansson (p. 253)
Book design by Lauryl Eddlemon
Cover design by RM Didier
Typeface: Myriad

10 9 8 7 6 5 4 3 2 1

For my beautiful daughter, Emma,

and my late brother, Rick.

Contents

Foreword

BY KEVIN PRICE

I am honored to be asked to write a foreword for Daniel Stewart's book *Pressure Proof Your Riding* and be part of his continued adventure to help focus the minds and thinking of riders in equestrian sports. Daniel is one of the most accomplished and energetic speakers I've met. His visually descriptive presentations thoroughly capture the attention of children and adults alike. I am therefore thrilled that he has undertaken the task of capturing his teachings in these pages.

I first met Daniel seven years ago at the USPC Annual Meeting in Kansas City, and even then, he was an accomplished presenter and teacher. Over the years I have had the opportunity to watch him present information in a fun and informative manner to help riders understand how to manage stress, think positively, set goals, and use visual techniques to help maximize success, enjoyment, and confidence while working with horses.

I am a firm believer in Daniel's message based on my own experience and learning to psychologically push through and forward during difficult times. I once shared with Daniel that at a three-day event in the spring of 1986, following challenging family events and the loss of a horse at an event the previous fall, I hummed Willie Nelson's "On the Road Again" from the start of roads-and-tracks straight through to my start on cross-country. Beyond that point, it was all a vision game as I had already successfully traversed the course and completed the obstacles at least a dozen times in my mind long before crossing the start flags.

I have no doubt there were at least a handful of volunteers on course that day that thought me a bit "touched" on hearing me hum "On the Road Again" as I rode along. However, it was the only way to calm my thoughts and allow myself to truly be in the present and to feel what was happening with "this" horse; and not allow myself to second guess, or as Daniel would say, allow "negative brain babble" to cloud my thoughts. Suffice to say, we had a successful day. I started the competition on a young unproven horse with the goal of finishing on a positive note and did so with a fifth place ribbon.

I'm not sure when I learned my positive thinking and visualization skills. Nonetheless, I am thankful to have learned them as they have served me well, both as a rider and in my professional life. I truly believe, regardless of your understanding of sport psychology, *Pressure Proof Your Riding* is an essential read. What I enjoy most in Daniel's message is its simplicity: quiet the brain babble; think and speak in the positive; remain calm, cool, and collected; and set goals to move ahead.

Kevin Price
CEO, US Pony Clubs

Introduction

BY LESLIE THRELKELD

On my first visit to the USEA Annual Meeting and Convention in 2011, Daniel Stewart's "Rider Strength and Conditioning Workshop" and "Equestrian Sports Psychology Seminar" were two of the most talked about items on the schedule. I attended the latter, where I did a bad job of taking notes for all the laughing we did instead. Daniel's enthusiasm is infectious, and his attitude toward emotional challenges makes having nerves and insecurities seem so normal—and so manageable.

Show jumping is the one phase of competitive eventing during which I get uncomfortable…I feel queasy and ill from start to finish. As a "cowabunga kid" I certainly didn't feel like I needed a handful of Tums prior to entering the ring. Somewhere along the way something changed. Maybe it's the pressure of becoming an adult who isn't as immune to criticism as a young rider on a scrappy little horse. Maybe I just don't want to let my horse down. As equestrians we tend to simply kick on and power through nervous feelings, but taking the opportunity to learn better methods of emotion management can give us all—riders, owners, spouses, and horses—a happier riding experience.

Daniel doesn't necessarily encourage abandoning nerves and insecurities altogether. He shows instead how they can be utilized and teaches you how to embrace emotional challenges and put them to good use. In this book, Daniel starts from square one by explaining the different types of pressures we experience as equestrians and the varying instinctual coping mechanisms that are often used. Then, sharing tools to promote positive and constructive emotions toward riding, he helps you create realistic goals and set yourself up for success. The text is easy to read and absorb, and Daniel's engaging character comes across without question, so you feel like you're having a constructive conversation with an encouraging friend.

Riders of every age and experience can benefit from *Pressure Proof Your Riding*, be it by learning a simple method of managing pressure or finding a new and improved attitude toward the mental facets of riding. At the very least, a reader will find inspiration in Daniel's optimistic outlook on getting the most out of life and his immeasurable passion for horses and horse people. Experience this book with an open mind and honest heart, and you may find out more about yourself and how you handle pressure than you may expect. Happy riding!

Leslie Threlkeld

Editor, Eventing USA
US Eventing Association

Acknowledgments

For the past 25 years I've had the pleasure of teaching thousands of hardworking riders, and I'd like to thank each and every one of them for the wonderful lessons they've taught me. As an educator, I've always believed that the best teachers are those who allow themselves to remain good students; to learn something valuable from everyone they meet. Much of the information in this book comes directly from the many wonderful students I've taught, so I thank them all for taking the time to teach this teacher.

I also want to express my gratitude to my family. Thank you to my wife Severine for her patience; to my children Luca and Emma for their encouragement; to my father for persuading me to write this book; to my mother for her constant support; and to my brother Ken for his kind words.

I'd like to share an especially heartfelt thanks to my late brother Rick: You were too young, and left us too early, but not before you taught me to believe in myself as a teacher, father, and family man. I miss you every day.

I'd also like to extend a special thanks to my artist, Erin Smith. Over the past decade I've watched her grow from a young rider to a successful and respected artist, and I'm proud and eternally grateful that she agreed to present her incredible talent in this book. I'd also like to thank all the wonderful riders who allowed me to use their photos. Without their consideration, *Pressure Proof Your Riding* would be in black-and-white—something that doesn't exist in riding—so I thank them for providing the lovely images that allow us all to see the wonderful color that horses bring to our lives.

I am also deeply grateful for the constant encouragement and indispensable support from my publishers, Trafalgar Square Books, especially from my publisher and editor Caroline Robbins for her never-ending assistance and hard work; Martha Cook for helping me understand how to bring it all together; and Rebecca Didier for helping me design—not only this book—but my entire *Pressure Proof* brand. I am indebted to the three of them and thank my lucky stars every day for their unwavering trust and confidence.

My final thanks go out to every horse I've ever had the pleasure and privilege of riding. Throughout the years they've taught me the importance of caring, patience, understanding, selflessness, and hard work. Every lesson has allowed me to grow into a more focused and confidant rider, teacher, husband, and father; and for that I am eternally grateful. I can only hope that the lessons I've taught horses and their riders, in turn, are equally as meaningful.

I've lost my mind...
and I'm pretty sure my horse took it!

Introduction to
Equestrian Sport Psychology

Physical training gives you a whole new <u>look</u>.
Mental training gives you a whole new <u>outlook</u>.

Acknowledging the Pressures of Riding

We riders are truly lucky because every day we get to do *what we love*. We spend time with horses, the one thing in our lives that often makes the most sense to us. Horses are our partners, friends, teachers, and sometimes even our therapists, and time with them today defines who we'll become tomorrow. Our sport is unlike any other because of the incredibly meaningful relationship between horse and rider. It's even more than a sport to us. It's our life: It's who we are, what we stand for, and why we do what we do.

As unique as our sport, is it has some similarities to other sports. These include (but are not limited to) pressure, stress, distraction, fear of failure, and performance anxiety, and they remind us that riding is, in fact, a true sport. Because of these common emotional challenges many of us struggle to *love what we do.* Sure we *do what we love,* but do we always *love what we do?* In a sport as special as ours we must do everything we can to ensure that negative emotions don't take away our positive experiences. We must do all we can to ensure that we love every second we spend on, around—or even underneath—our horses. In other words, we must do everything we can to become *Pressure Proof.*

In nature, when you plant a seed in the ground and nourish it, it will grow to be special and strong. Likewise, when you plant a seed of self-confidence, focus, or self-belief inside yourself and nourish it, you will also grow to be special and strong. In nature, good times always follow tough times: summer follows winter and sunny days follow rainy ones. The same thing happens in riding: *success* can always follow *disappointment; learning* can always follow a *mistake;* and *getting up* can always come after you've *fallen down.* You just need to believe that no matter how cloudy the skies of doubt or show jitters might look today, rays of confidence and success will still shine through tomorrow!

"Now, where did I leave my Confidence?"

Pressure Proof **Your Mind**

1 **Changing Stress into Success**

Chance are pretty good that you can recall a time when the pressure of showing made it difficult to compete at your best even though you'd ridden well all week in lessons. When the pressure went *up* your potential went *down.* In this situation, you have two ways of dealing with it. You can say, "What a shame. I was hoping to do well today," or you can say, "That's the last time I'm going to let pressure interfere with my ability to succeed."

Unfortunately, even when we vow to never let it happen again many of us just go home and continue doing what we've always done—working on our physical skills, forgetting that it wasn't our physical skills that let us down in the first place, but our mental reaction to pressure instead. Albert Einstein once said, "Insanity is doing the same thing over and over again and expecting a different result." Changing things up by adding a few mental-training exer-

All riders give some.
Some riders give all.

Watch Out for That Duck!

An eventer in the cross-country phase was having the ride of her life—leading after the dressage phase and great on time—that is, until she got hit in the chest by a duck! Unhurt, yet understandably distracted, the rider lost her focus and confidence, and ended up withdrawing for the day. Even though she had the physical skills to succeed (a great riding position, leg and seat), it was the mental distraction caused by the "duck to the chest" that prompted her to withdraw, proving that if you want to succeed in any situation, you'd be wise to train your brain along with your body.

Ever since that day, the "duck to the chest" has become a metaphor for "things that can limit your ability to succeed." For instance, negative self-talk like, "I can't do it," can be considered a "duck to the chest." Setting impossible goals, trying for the impossible (perfectionism), or fearing failure are some other "ducks" that can interfere with your ability to succeed. In order to ride your best, you're going to need to learn how to become *Pressure Proof* so that you can "*duck* the ducks"!

Being *Pressure Proof* means learning to keep it together when you'd normally fall apart.

cises to your mounted training program might be just what's needed to take a little of the insanity out of riding.

You can also probably recall a time when your riding performance fluctuated a lot: You rode well on Monday and Tuesday, not great on Wednesday, pretty well on Friday, and then poorly at the show over the weekend. What could cause these fluctuations? Studies show that our physical, technical, and athletic abilities don't change a great deal from one day to the next, so if they aren't responsible for these *performance fluctuations,* what are? The answer lies in mental skills—for example, focus, confidence, motivation, and an ability to cope with pressure, distraction, and adversity.

It happens all the time: A gifted dressage rider forgets her test because she's worried about what the judge is thinking. A young jumper pulls a rail because she can't get

The Most Important Distance of All

Distances such as 12-foot strides, 3-foot fences, and 450 meters per minute are important, but the most important distance of all is the 6 inches between your ears!

her head back into the game after falling in a previous class. A Western Pleasure rider gets nervous each time her husband watches her compete. These examples prove that there really is a connection between the physical and mental, and that the development of the *Pressure Proof* rider requires training for both the *body* and the *brain*.

Good physical rider + good mental rider = great rider.

There are two kinds of riders: those who welcome challenges, and those who don't. The *Pressure Proof* rider embraces challenges because she believes she can succeed, while the doubtful rider tries to avoid them because she's afraid she'll fail. The only real difference between these riders is that one has learned to be confident while the other hasn't.

None of us was born with a great deal of confidence or mental toughness. As babies we cried when we wanted something and we cried when we didn't. As small children we tried to get out of doing things we didn't like and tried to get into all sorts of things we shouldn't like! Only with time did we toughen up. This proves that mental strength is a skill that can be

Mental Coaching

Mental training isn't a mystery; there isn't a pill that'll help you handle pressure, or a stick you can shake to become more confident. It's a science, and like working with a strength-and-conditioning coach to achieve greater physical fitness, you can use the many techniques and tools developed by mental coaches to create greater mental fitness.

learned. You have the ability to develop good mental habits like rising above pressure, managing stress, and creating positive thoughts. These tools exist. You just need to know where the toolbox is and how to open it.

2 Clinical vs. Educational Sport Psychology

There are two kinds of sport psychology. *Clinical* sport psychology helps riders overcome mental challenges like depression, substance abuse, body image distortion, or eating disorders. This is not the kind I'll be discussing in this book. Instead I'll be writing about *educational* sport psychology—mental coaching that helps ordinary riders become extraordinary.

Most of us are ordinary: we get nervous under pressure and think of mistakes after making them. While this might be ordinary, it will most certainly interfere with your ability to ride your best. The goal of *educational sport psychology*, therefore, is to teach riders how to use mental skills like positive thinking, goal setting, stress management, and mental imagery so they can go from ordinary to extraordinary, from normal to super-normal.

The number one sign that a rider might need a little mental training is when pressure or show jitters makes it difficult for her to take her practice skills into show situations. Dwelling on past mistakes; worrying about letting others down (or not living up to their expectations); being easily distracted or quickly frustrated; having feelings of perfectionism and fear of failure all contribute to pressure and performance anxiety. These

Super Normal

Mental Training

It helps you to:

- Improve your confidence and composure.
- Replace self-doubt with self-belief.
- Handle pressure so you can ride to your ability.
- Overcome performance anxiety or show jitters.
- Develop greater motivation.
- Sharpen your focus and concentration.
- Increase your mental toughness.
- Block out distractions.
- Make skills more effective and consistent.
- Bounce back from adversity.
- Overcome mental blocks like forgetting courses and tests.
- Identify limiting factors like doubt and indecision that hold you back.
- Maintain an even temperament regardless of pressure.
- Find and feel more enjoyment in your riding.

are all signs that sport psychology can help. Other signs include starting out poorly and not being able to finish strong; starting strongly and letting it slip away; riding *down* to the level of the competition; being in a slump; choking; and not having fun. There's no shortage of reasons to consider *mental coaching*, and thankfully, there's no shortage of mental-training tools to help.

Emotions shouldn't get the best of you. They should get the best out of you!

3 "Driven" Types of Riders

Fear and Outcome Driven

Just like our fingerprints, as humans we're all unique: We have strengths and weaknesses that make us special and define who we are. Often, the greatest difference between good riders and great riders is what drives and motivates them. The *fear-driven* rider wants very badly to succeed but lacks the self-confidence to believe in her ability. Instead of focusing on what she believes *can* happen, she focuses on what she's afraid *might* happen.

The *outcome-driven* rider also lacks the ability to focus on what she believes, and simply bases her self-worth on the outcome of her rides. Instead of feeling good about her performances, she focuses on standings (whom she beat and who beat her) and, as a result, worries a great deal about losing, or embarrassing herself, or not living up to others' expectations. Obviously, *fear-driven* and *outcome-driven* mindsets are detrimental to performance.

"What if I forget my test, fall off, and lose my mind?!"

Success-Driven

A third kind of rider is called *success-driven,* and unlike the other two, this rider focuses on what she must do in order to ride well. She doesn't focus on the boulders blocking her path but, instead, figures out how to climb on top of them so she can have a better view. She's able to maintain a positive outlook because she embraces challenges as much as she embraces success. She loves the battle as much as the victory. She is *Pressure Proof!*

Like a toddler who falls a million times but refuses to give up, *success-driven* riders keep on pushing even when challenges seem insurmountable. Everything to a toddler is an opportunity to learn: bumping into things, knocking things over, and falling down are just temporary setbacks in his quest for improvement. The same is true for the success-driven rider. (For more information on *fear-* and *success-driven* riders, please see p. 49.)

The only rider you need to be better than today, is the rider you were yesterday.

Feelers vs. Doers

Riders can be classified in two other interesting ways. *Feelers* are those who make an effort only when they feel like it (when it's convenient and easy) and make no effort when they *don't* feel like it (when it's inconvenient or hard). The opposite of *feelers* are *doers:* Riders who embrace challenges and refuse to let short-term discomfort, fatigue, or exertion derail their efforts to achieve greatness. They believe in their ability and take responsibility for mistakes or missed opportunities and are, therefore, able to learn from them. Evolving from a *feeler* to a *doer* is just as important as evolving from the trot to the canter, or from the *fear-* or *outcome-driven* mindset to the *success-driven* mindset.

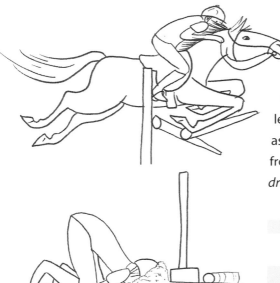

It's not how often you fall down but how fast you get back up.

Cognitive Miser

To achieve greatness you must believe you're capable of attaining it. Instead of doing whatever it takes to achieve greatness, a "cognitive miser" feels incapable of success and, therefore, only exerts a minimum amount of mental effort. In order to avoid becoming this kind of miser, always know that you are capable; believe in yourself; give 100 percent; and never give up—regardless of the challenge.

4 Developing a Pressure Proof Plan

One of the biggest mistakes any rider can make is not having any mental plan at all. You wouldn't prepare for a show without a physical plan and you shouldn't prepare for one without a mental plan either. All too often a rider works hard on developing a strong leg, seat, and position only to see it all crumble under the weight of a little pressure. We're all humans (and therefore imperfect) and will struggle with pressure from time to time. As a matter of fact, even the world's greatest riders feel pressure on occasion. What makes them so great, however, is that they're able to identify what's causing it and create a plan of action to overcome it.

The most effective way to do it, is to <u>do it</u>.

Focusing on physical preparation, but ignoring mental preparation means that a rider is only willing to go half the distance. As a result, when pressure goes up a rider's position, potential, performance, and possibilities all seem to go down. You can avoid this by *planning your ride* (mentally and physically) and then *riding your plan*.

Identify Your Strengths and Weaknesses

The first step to creating a *Pressure Proof* plan is to identify your strengths and weaknesses. This is called *cognitive*

What to Include in a **Pressure Proof Plan**

- Focus on yourself rather than your opponent—focus on the best, not the rest.
- Learn to love challenges instead of avoiding them.
- Avoid letting daily stressors become a distraction—riding should distract you instead.
- Focus on the present rather than on the past or future; don't allow past mistakes or future potential standings interfere with *right now.*
- Most importantly, always remember to have fun.

appraisal and is necessary before you can move on. Think back in time to a lesson or show when things didn't go as planned. How did you respond emotionally? Without this kind of self-evaluation, you can't really identify a starting point, and without a starting point, there can't really be a finish line. The ancient Greeks knew this well and proved it by inscribing the words *Gnothi Seautonon* on the

KNOW THYSELF

tip   How to Create Different Plans **for Different Challenges**

Plan A: The Normal Plan.
Write down everything you need to do—both physical and mental—to perform your best during a ride or show. It's important to include a plan for the night before; the morning of; 30 minutes before; 10 minutes before; and one minute before you start. For example:

- *Night before:* Use a relaxation technique to ensure a good night's sleep.

- *First thing in the morning:* Listen to motivating music to pump yourself up.

- *30 minutes before mounting:* Recall a positive riding memory from your past.

- *10 minutes before mounting:* Use mental imagery to visualize your ride.

- *One minute before mounting:* Repeat a few positive affirmation sentences.

- *Ready to go:* Take a few deep breaths and smile as you enter the arena.

Plan B: The Quickie Plan
This variation of Plan A is used when you have a limited amount of time to prepare for your ride or show. Arriving late and misplacing your helmet is a good example of when to use this plan. Since you have very little time, simply select the physical and mental skills you feel are most important to your preparation—those that can be done quickly. You could repeat a positive affirmation sentence or motto; think of a line from your favorite song; and take two deep breaths to keep the pressure at bay.

Plan C: The Hurry-Up-and-Wait Plan
Another variation of Plan A, this helps you cope with unexpected *delays* prior to riding

Temple of Apollo at Delphi. Directly translated it means "Know Thyself."

When developing your *Pressure Proof* plan it's important to take into consideration the two different kinds of stress: *Cognitive stress* refers to the mental tension that occurs in your mind such as frustration, anxiety, and nervousness. *Somatic stress* refers to the mental tension that occurs in your body like disrupted

Sport psychology gives you a checkup from the neck up!

sleep or eating patterns, headaches, cramps, or a nervous stomach. The reason you must focus on both types is because your mind and body are

or showing. Often times, a rider completes her mental preparations right on time only to find that the previous rider has broken a fence on course and the maintenance crew will need 10 minutes for repair. It's at times like this that you really need to keep your head squarely on your shoulders so when creating this "delay plan," it's important to have a clear idea of which physical and mental skills keep you most focused and sharp. For example, your plan could include dismounting; stretching; listening to a motivating song; and doing a few mental rehearsals of your course or test.

Plan D: The "Oh, Crap" Plan

What can you do when you've done everything right but things still go wrong? This is where the "Oh, Crap" Plan comes in. Designed to help you stay confident when things are going poorly so that you can quickly find a productive solution, and therefore, an end to the problem, it should contain a

series of quick mental "tools" to help you stay focused when you find yourself in the middle of a ride yelling, "Oh, crap"! As soon as you hear yourself saying these words (or any other similar expletive) quickly initiate this pre-determined plan, which could include thinking of a *positive self-image statement* (p. 130); recalling a *positive memory* when you successfully handled a similar situation (p. 160); or repeating a *motivating motto* like "If it's going to be, it's up to me" (p. 128). This plan is especially important after a major disruption like a fall; run-out; refusal; spook; or a momentarily forgotten course or test. Remember, it's not just the disruption that's the problem, it's that you don't always know what to do when it happens.

"Oh, Crap!"

linked. It's impossible for a worried and anxious mind to exist in a calm and relaxed body. It's also impossible for a worried and anxious body to exist with a calm and relaxed mind, which means that when you can develop a calm and relaxed mind, your body will follow suit. What happens between your ears affects what happens below them!

Feel It to Fix It

This is a phrase used to describe the importance of being aware of a weakness before you can overcome it (if you can *feel* it, you can *fix* it). Unfortunately, when you're unaware of your imperfections you probably don't know what needs improving. Physically, you do this every time you ride by feeling your leg swing at the canter or feeling yourself bounce while sitting the trot. When you feel these imperfections you can set a plan to overcome them (riding without stirrups, for example). The same rule applies to becoming *Pressure Proof*: When you *feel* yourself responding to pressure by becoming frustrated, angry, or disappointed, you're actually well on your way to *fixing* it.

Riding without a plan is like trying to dig out of a hole using a shovel instead of a rope.

You can't fix what you can't face.

5 There's No "Self" in Centered Riding

I've always said that whatever you want to create in your horse you should first create it in yourself. To create a straight and balanced horse, you must first create a straight and balanced rider. Likewise, to create confidence and focus in your horse you must first create confidence and focus in yourself. The mental and physical traits you wish for your horse are all within your reach as long as you hold yourself to the same expectations.

One of the biggest mistakes a rider can make is to believe that she's separate from her horse (two athletes working *apart* toward the same goal). There's no "I" in this team and there's no "self" in *Centered Riding* (being *self-centered* limits your ability to learn from your horse). Success in our sport only comes when horse and rider work together. You never see a player in a doubles tennis team at Wimbledon constantly yelling at his partner or hitting him with his racquet. If this happened that team would never have become good enough to qualify for Wimbledon. When they don't play well together, their chance of success diminishes. The same thing goes for

A horse and rider may not have it all together, but together they have it all.

riding: If you don't play well with your horse, you'll never succeed, but when you play well with him, your chance of success goes up. When this actually happens, it often feels like you:

- Have supreme confidence in your ability.
- Maintain focus at a high level regardless of the challenge.
- Have a sense of knowing that you can do what's needed.
- Ride well regardless of pressure or adversity.
- Stay persistent and positive when things go wrong.
- Believe you're competitive, confident, concentrated, composed and in control.
- Are a positive and responsible partner for your horse.
- Are *Pressure Proof*…and so is your horse!

6 Young Rider Sport Psychology

Mental training can help all riders regardless of age. Many trainers and coaches start introducing sport psychology as early as age seven or eight —sometimes even earlier—with the idea that the sooner they plant good *mental seeds* the better chance they'll have of growing. When young riders learn early to think positively, manage stress, develop self-esteem, strengthen their confidence, set reasonable goals, and overcome mental challenges like pressure and show jitters, they'll have a much greater chance of riding well throughout their entire lives.

Learn to "just do it" instead of "just undo it."

Preventive vs. Corrective Medicine

Mental coaching for the young rider can be considered *preventive medicine* because it teaches her tools to handle emotional challenges before they actually happen. When teachers wait too long—teaching the tools after the challenges have affected the rider—it becomes *corrective medicine,* which means having to break down the bad habits and replace them with more productive ones. It's never too early or too late to start a mental-training program, but while the phrase "Just *do* it" might work well for those who start early, it might need to be changed to "Just *undo* it" for those who wait too long.

It's important that a mental-training program doesn't put any additional pressure on a rider—young or old—so it's best to start with no more than an hour a week (perhaps split into two 30-minute sessions). Since many riders incorrectly base their self-worth on the total amount of their show or schooling successes, it's important that any mental-training program teach them to judge themselves based on their progress, skill development, and the relationship they create with their horse and riding mates.

Role of the Parent and Trainer

The role of the parent and trainer is a pivotal one. Both need to be supportive without becoming overly involved, assist the young rider in setting goals without making them their own, and help him or her manage expectations by not setting the bar too high. If they forget any of these there's a good chance the young rider will feel self-doubt and disappointment. This is called the *confidence/expectation connection:* when expectations go up, confidence often goes down.

Bring up the young rider without putting her down.

Praise

Praise plays an important role in a young rider's mental training. Youngsters have a hunger for realistic evaluations so it's important that praise be well deserved and sincere (avoid praising when they know they haven't done well). The young rider also accepts praise best when it focuses on specific goal achievement and when it's somewhat infrequent. *Constant* praise seems to lessen its message and lower its value, while *specific* and *infrequent* praise helps riders learn what skills allowed them to succeed—or not.

One interesting method of delivering praise is called *sandwiching.* Instead of delivering praise only, you sandwich one piece of constructive criticism between two pieces of praise. In this way, young riders develop self-confidence and pride but still understand that there's more out there for them to learn. "You had great focus on course today, you still got a little tense in the start box, but I love how you finished strong," is an example that shows how praise alone might not deliver enough of a message—it's actually the criticism in the middle that's the most constructive.

The best teachers tell their students where to look but don't tell them what to see.

Likewise, *continuous* praise may also give the young rider the incorrect idea that she's reached the limits of her ability, while infrequent praise along with periodic constructive criticism conveys the message that she can still improve. Yes, you want to praise the young rider, but forgetting to give her something to work on will only limit how far she can go. Sooner or later, you'll need to push her out of the nest to see if she can fly.

It's also important that praise focus on *measurable* and *repeatable* skills the young rider has control over. When you praise in a way that says, "You did well because you're so talented," the student might shy away from future challenges because it could threaten her self-esteem: "If I don't do well next time does it mean I'm no longer talented?" "You did well because you stayed so focused," emphasizes something that the rider has control over and something she can re-create in the future.

tip

How to Be a Good Young Rider **Mental Coach**

- "Warm" riders to the idea of mental training rather than forcing them into it. The harder you push, the harder they can push back.

- Remind them that mental coaching increases success by increasing the amount of enjoyment they'll feel.

- Use the words *mental training* instead of *sport psychology*. The word "psychology" might make them feel as if there's something wrong with them.

- Make mental coaching fun and even humorous so they'll enjoy, embrace, and retain it. We always learn the most from teachers who amuse us.

- Teach age-appropriate tools like allowing them to listen to motivating music instead of telling them to turn their music off.

- Keep a written record of their goals and other tools (like a list of their favorite songs) so you can remind them when they forget.

- Help build team cohesion between them and their riding mates. Riding always feels better when done with people we enjoy being around.

- Be careful of "labels." For example, introducing a young rider as "Ms. Perfect" may unintentionally create unwanted pressure on her to live up to the name.

- Focus on what they do really well in addition to what they're struggling with. Avoid only picking out mistakes *or* constantly giving unearned praise.

- Help them identify and appreciate their strengths and teach them to avoid comparing themselves to others.

- Teach them to measure their success by the effort they give rather than the score they get.

- Avoid coaching from the sidelines as it often makes young riders feel anxious. Instead, catch them doing something well and praise them with a simple smile or congratulatory thumbs up.

- Find coachable moments to use as life lessons such as the importance of responsibility, good sportsmanship, coping with adversity, and working well with others.

7 Common Misconceptions

The goal of *Pressure Proofing* is to match a strong body with an equally strong mind, and set the conditions that will allow you to ride your best every time. Even though it makes sense, there are still a few misconceptions that hold some riders back from giving mental training a try.

Learn the Truth about Many Mental Coaching "Myths"

FICTION: Mental training only helps riders with problems.
FACT: Mental training is about helping ordinary riders become extraordinary.

FICTION: Mental training only focuses on overcoming weaknesses.
FACT: Mental training actually helps you identify your strengths and use them to ride your best.

FICTION: Mental weaknesses are genetic and you can't change them.
FACT: Weaknesses (such as low confidence) are not hereditary and can be improved.

FICTION: Mental training only improves your riding.
FACT: Mental training can also make you more confident in school, at work, and in your relationships.

FICTION: Mental training is only for elite riders.
FACT: Mental training can help all riders regardless of age, levels, disciplines, or mindsets.

Without a strong mental plan you might feel "lost" and out of control, but sport psychology can act like a beacon in a storm, helping you regain control and move forward toward your potential. Without confidence, riders just seem to tread water and make no headway; they get knocked around by each passing wave and barely keep their head above the surface. *Pressure Proofing* gives you the tools you need to find your direction in any storm; instead of simply treading water, it allows you to make waves!

Measure your success by the effort you give rather than the score you get.

Big shots are just little shots who kept on shooting.

PRESSURE PROOF PROJECT

Rate Your Mental Mindset

Answer the following questions using the key below to determine if *mental training* can help you improve your riding:

0 = Never   1 = Sometimes   2 = Almost Always

_____ I'm driven by success rather than by fear (of not achieving success) or by outcomes.

_____ I'm a *doer,* not a *feeler* (I do things when it's necessary, not only when I feel like it).

_____ I know my strengths and weaknesses and use this knowledge to improve.

_____ I embrace my imperfections and know that I must *feel* them in order to fix them.

_____ I always plan my ride—and ride my plan; I have plans for delays and when I'm rushed.

_____ I always respect and treat my horse as an equal partner.

_____ I know that it's never too soon or too late to start a mental-training program.

_____ I believe that mental weaknesses are not permanent; I can learn to improve them.

_____ I believe that mental training can help me in my normal life—in addition to my riding.

_____ I believe that mental training can take me from ordinary to extraordinary.

_____ **Total** (add up your answers).

If your score added up to:

14 to 20

Great! You've learned the value of mental training and can use it effectively. There's always room for improvement so continue to think about what you've read in this chapter.

8 to 13

You're on the right track but need more to do more work to ensure mental training can help you. Make a list of your greatest mental challenges and start improving them using the tools in this book.

0 to 7

You struggle with your mental game and need a mental-training program to gain control of it. Read this chapter again very carefully and formulate your plan of action.

2
Defense Mechanisms

"What lies behind you and what lies before you pale in comparison to what lies inside you."
—Ralph Waldo Emerson

Three Types of Emotions

There are three common kinds of emotions: (1) *productive*—like confidence and self-belief—that lay the foundation for success; (2) *destructive*—like show jitters and fear of failure—that hold you back from succeeding; and (3) *protective*—like avoidance and denial—that never give you the chance to succeed in the first place.

As a rider, you're free to choose the kind of emotions you ride with. In the face of a challenge, you can choose to be: confident, optimistic, composed, and happy; nervous, tense, anxious, and miserable; or avoid the challenge altogether. This last choice is a part of a group of *protective emotions* called *defense mechanisms,* and it is these emotions that I'm going to discuss in this chapter.

To get something you've never had, be prepared to do something you've never done.

Universal Emotions

Surprise, fear, disgust, anger, happiness, sadness, and contempt are considered *universal emotions* because they exist in all humans regardless of race, age, skin color, religion, country, language, or culture. So, the next time you feel one of them—even if it's negative like *fear* or *anger*—don't feel too bad because you're not alone! Everyone else in the entire world has felt it, too. This doesn't mean you shouldn't work to overcome it; it just means you're human.

Pressure Proof **Your Protective Emotions**

1 Defense Mechanisms

Defense mechanisms are called *protective emotions* because they can momentarily reduce the amount of anxiety, disappointment, or risk you might feel. Unfortunately, when you avoid a challenge you interfere with your ability to overcome it. There are many different causes of defense mechanisms, but they usually all come down to *reasons* and *results:* We always have great *reasons* for *why* we don't go for great *results*. Instead of playing the winning game, we play the *blame game*, blaming everything from our horse, tack, or judges, to the bad economy for not riding well. (We'd even blame the weather if we could just forget that it also rains on confident riders!)

Success is a matter of choice, not a matter of chance.

A *defense mechanism* can be as mild as avoidance or procrastination, or as serious as fear. An example of a *fear-based* defense mechanism is when an unpleasant past experience reminds you to avoid letting it happen again in the future—for example, when the knob on the tackroom door always gives you a static shock, sooner or later you learn to anticipate and avoid reaching for it. This is called *adverse thinking*: Instead of spending your time figuring out how to solve the problem, you spend time trying to figure out how to avoid it altogether, even though holding a towel when opening the door— or changing the doorknob—would simply solve the problem.

Identify whether you have the tendency to use any of the following defense mechanisms:

"I didn't forget to tighten my girth, it just happened!"

- **Denial**—Refusing to take responsibility for something by saying it never happened. "I didn't forget to tighten my girth."

- **Avoidance**—Decreasing the amount of discomfort you might feel by avoiding the situation all together. "I probably won't win so I'll just withdraw my entry now."

- **Indecision**—Struggling between two or more options resulting in an inability to give 100 percent to any of them. "I can't decide whether I should jump the oxer, stay with the vertical, or just withdraw."

- **Repression**—Coping with negative emotions by pushing them from your mind. "I don't know what you're talking about, I never get nervous riding in front of crowds."

> **"Never leave till tomorrow what you can do today."**
> – Benjamin Franklin

I used to be indecisive, but now I'm not sure...

- **Projection**—Feeling negative emotions but attributing them to someone else. "I'm not the one in a bad mood, it's my parents, trainer, judge (insert your scapegoat here)."

  - **Procrastination**—Putting off actions until tomorrow when you can do them today. "I just fell off, so I should probably take a break and get back on tomorrow."

Don't blame the arrow in your arm, blame the person who shot it!

- **Rationalization**—Using protective thoughts to explain away negative feelings.

- **Tanking**—Making excuses so that disappointments don't seem so overwhelming. "I didn't win today because I didn't care. If I cared, I would have done better."

Someday is not a day of the week.

- **Withdrawal**—Expending as little mental energy as possible. "I always get nervous riding for judges so why should I even try."

- **Displacement**—Directing negative emotions toward something else like throwing gloves or smacking the horse. "It doesn't make things better, but it makes me feel better."

  - **Anticipation**—Lessening the potential of a disappointment by blaming something before starting. "I have a bad headache so I wouldn't be surprised if I ride horribly."

    - **Helplessness**—Demanding assistance from others or believing something is impossible even though you haven't tried it yet. "There's no way I can do this, I just know it."

"That would have gone better if my reins weren't so slippery!"

- **Surrender**—Giving up on the present because of the past. "Every time I compete against her she always wins so why should I even try?"

- **Distraction**—Purposely scheduling something at the same time as what you're trying to avoid. "I can't ride for that mean judge because I have to meet with my vet then."

Uh-oh...

Causes of Defense Mechanisms

There are many different causes and each one can interfere with your ability to become *Pressure Proof*. They include, but are not limited to, doubt, uncertainty, low confidence, poor willpower, and a lack of self-belief. The rationale behind them always comes down to something like, "If I wait, it might get easier," and "If I deny it's happening, it might not bother me as much," or "If I blame it on someone else, people won't lower their opinion of me." Unfortunately, delaying *productive* tasks in favor of *protective* excuses always leads to underperformance, disappointment, low self-esteem, and unrealized goals.

> There are three kinds of riders: Those who make things happen; those who watch things happen; and those who wonder what just happened.

Another cause of defense mechanisms is *inaction*— that is, *waiting* for things to happen instead of *making* them happen. (Ever notice that when you wait for a call, the phone never rings, or when you wait for Mr. Right only Mr. Wrong seems to come around?) Instead of *inaction*, believe in yourself and find the courage to choose *action*. Other reasons for your defense mechanisms include:

- **Having Too Many Choices**—When facing many equal yet challenging options it's often easier to just choose answer "D" (none of the above).

To protect yourself from making the wrong decision (or the hard one) you simply decide *not* to decide—that is, you choose *not* to choose. Choices can be hard. After all, if you have a hard time choosing between green or blue polo wraps or rubber versus braided reins, imagine how hard it can be to decide if you really want to jump a four-foot-high wooden goose or compete in front of a stadium full of spectators. It's normal to struggle from time to time with important and challenging decisions, but it's also normal to believe in your ability to accomplish them.

Pressure shouldn't get the best <u>of</u> you—it should get the best <u>out of</u> you.

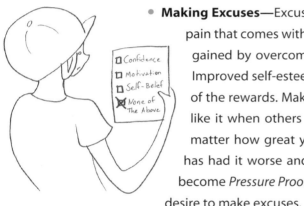

- **Making Excuses**—Excuse-making may lessen some of the short-term pain that comes with disappointment, but the long-term positives gained by overcoming a challenge *far* outweigh any negatives. Improved self-esteem, self-confidence, and self-respect are a few of the rewards. Making excuses is a *self-defeating* habit; we don't like it when others do it, so let's not engage in it ourselves. No matter how great your favorite excuse is, someone somewhere has had it worse and has succeeded in spite of it. You'll learn to become *Pressure Proof* when your desire for success surpasses your desire to make excuses.

- **Resisting Change**—Change is necessary for improvement, but it's not always easy. Working to your strengths is important, but you must also have the courage to identify your weaknesses and want to change them. One thing that makes it difficult to embrace change is that going against the *status quo* is very often met with resistance. Sometimes the effort to make a change is just as hard as the problem causing it. It's as if you're being tested to see if you're really serious about making the positive change: You vow to start a diet and later that day find your mailbox stuffed full of restau-

There's no remote control for riding; get up and change it yourself.

rant coupons, photos of ice cream, and an invitation to a cocktail party. Perhaps this is why of the millions of people who resolve to lose weight on New Year's Eve, only about 14 percent actually follows through. It's not because it's impossible, it's just because change is very hard. Some change can be undeniably stressful—it's what puts divorce, moving, marriage, and even childbirth at the top of the list of the most stressful events in our lives. What makes these events so difficult is that the change is often unexpected

A turtle only makes progress when he sticks his neck out.

and usually more than we bargained for. Even adjusting to smaller changes—like moving up from a pony to a horse—requires energy and effort. In order to embrace change, remind yourself that you're in it for the long term. Persistence and preparation are two keys to becoming *Pressure Proof*.

- **Hanging On to Preconceived Notions**—Negative thoughts and beliefs can hold you back from riding your best. "I've never ridden well in this arena so I know I won't ride well here today, either," or "My warm-up was horrible so I know I won't ride well in my class," are two examples of a *preconceived notion*. Instead of creating your own destiny, you believe you're limited by it and nothing can change it. To rise above preconceived notions you need to remind yourself, "I

The Four-Minute Mile

Not so very long ago, it was believed that running a mile in under four minutes was impossible. This *preconceived notion* took root in the running world and stayed true for years. Runners believed it was impossible so they never aimed for it or even imagined beating it. That was until May 6, 1954, when British athlete Roger Bannister went out and proved it wrong. By refusing to accept the *preconceived notion,* he pushed himself to a point where others didn't dare go, and in doing so, created one of the greatest success stories in all of sports. Interestingly, immediately after he broke the four-minute mark, numerous other runners started to beat it as well. As soon as the preconceived notion was removed, so were the limitations.

don't have to win the warm-up." You can actually struggle from time to time and still succeed.

To get whatever you want, be prepared to do whatever it takes.

- **Staying in Your Comfort Zone**—*Preconceived notions* can also create something called a *comfort zone*, the belief that you're capable of only a certain amount of success and when you reach that level, you've gone as far as you can go. "I never finish better than fourth so that's probably where I'll finish today." Sadly, when you set these kinds of "expectation-based limits" you hold yourself back from really giving or getting 100 percent. Overcoming your *comfort zone* requires taking risks and while living *within* it might feel comfortable—setting the bar so low you can trip over it—the true sign of a *Pressure Proof* rider is one who identifies a risk and pushes toward it by raising the bar just a touch higher. Along with this may come the risk of not reaching the bar, but the confident rider never lets this hold her back; instead she stays focused on what she's capable of and never doubts herself or gives up.

tip
How to Stop Making Excuses

- Make a *no-excuse zone* in your horse trailer or an empty stall, for example. These are the places where you're not allowed to make excuses, procrastinate, withdraw, or surrender.
- Learn to enjoy taking full responsibility for your actions. When the water bucket is empty, fill it; when the stall is dirty, clean it; and when you make a mistake, own it.
- Adopt a *no-excuse attitude* and go public with your decision by telling others. This will help you feel more confident and create a feeling of accountability.
- Surround yourself with other riders who've also adopted a *no-excuse attitude.*
- Develop a *do-it-now attitude* so you won't have time to doubt yourself or look for excuses.
- Learn to never feel sorry for and always believe in yourself.

Scarcity vs. Abundance Mindsets

When it comes to riding you can make plans for tomorrow instead of doing them today; you can focus on doing what's easy instead of doing what's

Success starts at the end of your comfort zone.

hard; and you can dwell on your mistakes instead of learning from them. When you do this you develop something called a *scarcity mindset:* an attitude where you're only aware of what you *don't* have or what you *don't* want to have happen.

The opposite of this negative mindset is an *abundance mindset:* an attitude where you're aware of what you *do* have; what you *do* want to achieve; and what you *do* need to do to accomplish it. When it comes to avoiding defense mechanisms there are only two simple rules:

Rule 1: Never make excuses or give up.
Rule 2: Always follow Rule 1.

PRESSURE PROOF PROJECT

Rate Your Confidence

Answer the following questions to determine if *confidence training* can help you become more *Pressure Proof*.

0 = Never   1 = Sometimes   2 = Almost Always

_____ I am always optimistic, never pessimistic.

_____ I never blame my horse, the judge, or others for troubles, mistakes, or missed opportunities.

_____ I never avoid things just because they're difficult or inconvenient.

_____ I never procrastinate; I do things now instead of waiting for them to get easier.

_____ I never make excuses.

_____ Making decisions is easy for me.

_____ I embrace change.

_____ I have no preconceived notions about my limitations.

_____ I always focus on what I have, not on what I don't have.

_____ I'm not afraid to push myself outside my mental comfort zone.

_____ **Total** (add up your answers).

If your score added up to:

14 to 20

Great—you've learned the value of confidence and can use it effectively. There's always room for improvement so continue to think about what you've read in this chapter.

8 to 13

You're on the right track but need more training to make you a more confident rider. Make a list of the challenges that bother you the most and start to improve them by using the tools outlined here.

0 to 7

You have low confidence and need a mental-training program to improve it. Read this chapter again very carefully and make a sensible plan forward.

3
Positive Mental Traits

*You can't go back and start a new beginning, but
you can start now to make a new ending.*

There's No <u>Wrong</u> Way to Do the <u>Right</u> Thing

Positive *emotions* create positive *motions:* It's impossible for your body to ride in a tense and rushed way, full of self-doubt, when your mind is confident, positive, and focused. What goes on between your ears affects what happens below them; what's going through your mind goes through your body. If you're mentally tense, you'll ride in a physically tense way, and no matter how you add it up, these two wrongs never make a right.

There's a true connection between your mind and body so how well your body works, depends on how well your mind works. The many tools, techniques, and tips discussed throughout this book are designed to help you create the many mental attributes that will help you become *Pressure Proof*. I will be discussing these positive attributes in this chapter.

Pressure Proof **Your Mental Strengths**

1 **Develop Self-Confidence**

Also known as "self-efficacy," *self-confidence* is perhaps the strongest and most powerful of all mental attributes. When you feel confident you believe in your ability to succeed and soar over hurdles instead of crashing into them. This is called a *self-serving bias*—you choose to believe in yourself instead of choosing to doubt yourself, and the result is almost always a more positive and productive ride. Your *emotions* really do control your *motions.*

<u>No</u> confidence and <u>no</u> success; or <u>know</u> confidence and <u>know</u> success.

Self-confidence can come from many sources including:

- **Past Accomplishments**—Having set yourself challenging goals in the past—and achieved them—makes you feel like you can achieve them again in the future.

Pressure Proof Attributes

Self-Confidence	Arousal	Consistency
Positive Self-Image	In the Zone	Optimism
Concentration	Focus on the Present	Self-Belief
Motivation	Accountability	Composure
Mental Toughness	Initiative	Resilience
Focus on the Solution	Passion	Self-Esteem
Trust	Commitment	
	Patience	

- **Verbal Persuasion**—Receiving positive and reinforcing comments from coaches, parents, teachers (or yourself through positive thinking) can create confidence.

- **Imagined Experiences**—Visualizing you're riding well—*and* succeeding—can help you create a mental blueprint, leading to a feeling of self-belief.

Ever notice that when a loving couple argues they never throw the good china? It's because they know that there will always be another day.

- **Emotional State**—Being in a positive mood (instead of feeling worried or nervous) helps unleash the emotions that are needed to ride your best.

Improving your *self-confidence* improves the likelihood that you'll become *Pressure Proof*. The many techniques described in this book are designed for that very reason. For example, *stress management* increases confidence by teaching you how to cope with and control stress; *toughness training* increases confidence by teaching you how to act courageously in challenging situations; and *positive thinking* increases confidence by teaching you how to replace negative and limiting thoughts with positive and empowering ones.

When confidence is Number One everything else just seems to add up.

Rule 120

Giving 100 percent creates a *good* rider, but push yourself to give 120 percent and you'll create a *great* one. This means that when your trainer asks you to ride for five minutes without stirrups, you push to give her six minutes; and when she asks you to arrive on time, you arrive a few minutes early. Always seek out a way to give 20 percent more than asked: Drop your stirrups even when you don't have to; video

Go ahead and take the stirrups off my saddle for the week!

Focus on what you can control: yourself.

Control Yourself!

Riders are control freaks. We try to control a 1,000-pound animal, the judges, and even the weather! We should just stick with what we *can* control—ourselves.

a lesson and watch it later; visualize your ride before you enter the arena; or pick up manure even when it's not your job. In the end, you'll develop the feeling that you're a confident rider who's always capable of giving more than what is asked.

2 Ride with a Positive Self-Image

Your self-image is the blueprint that determines how you'll behave; what you'll try; what you'll avoid; and who you'll become. It's a subconscious mechanism that controls your behavior just like a thermostat controls room temperature. It guides and directs your actions and behaviors until your self-image becomes a reality.

What you see is ultimately what you'll get: Your every thought and action stems from the way you see yourself, and the image you form is influenced by your past riding experiences, successes, failures, and the many thoughts you have about yourself. In other words, *you are who you believe you are;* what you put into it is what you get out of it.

To get the most <u>out of it</u>, be prepared to put the most <u>into it</u>.

When you see yourself as confident and capable, you're going to have a great day, but if you see yourself as hopelessly unsuccessful, it might just be a very long and frustrating one. You just can't expect to behave differently from your self-image. It would be like putting an apple pie in the oven and an hour later thinking you'll pull out a chocolate cake: You can't *believe* you're going to ride poorly and still ride well.

Developing a strong self-image begins with the belief that you're capable of accomplishing great things. When you believe in yourself, your self-image motivates and drives you toward your potential. When you improve your self-image, you improve your attitude; when you improve your attitude, you improve your actions; and when you improve your

Confirmation Bias

When you believe something to be true (even if it's negative) you often become biased, believing that there's nothing you can do about it. For example, if you believe everyone's better than you, you might not give 100 percent. In the end, you don't ride as well as you could because you've convinced yourself that it wouldn't make a difference. This is called *confirmation bias*: the *bias* (not being as good as everyone else) is *confirmed* (by not trying as hard). In the end, it's very common for riders like this to say, "See, I was right. Everyone is better than me."

In order to avoid negative *confirmation bias*, always keep an open mind. You limit your possibilities when you believe things are the way they are and that nothing can change them. People who believe that airplanes are dangerous (even though flying has been proven to be much safer than driving) will continue to have a fear of flying until they overcome their bias. Likewise, riders who always think they'll never be any good, or that they're not as good as others, will continue to ride below their potential until they overcome *their* bias.

actions, you improve the likelihood of success. Here are a few signs that your self-image could use a little improvement:

- Frequent jealousy, frustration, guilt, or self-criticism.

- Unintentional negative self-talk and constant comparisons of yourself to others.

- An inability to give or accept compliments, or feeling that you're undeserving of success.

Attitude of Gratitude

A healthy self-image allows you to accept and value compliments from others knowing that, as with any gift, it would be rude not to accept them. You don't have to be perfect to accept a compliment with a graceful thank you. Successful riders do it all the time because they know it's healthy to acknowledge a job well done. If you congratulate Karen O'Conner, George Morris, or Steffen Peters you won't hear them say, "It was a fluke," or "It

"Yes, but …."

Children have a strange ability to turn any conversation into one about "butts": Yours is funny, hers wiggles, and his is big! It's cute as kids, but just as children are expected to grow out of the *"butt"* phase, we should also be expected to grow out of the *"yes, but…"* phase.

Turn a compliment into confidence.

was an accident." They'll just thank you because they've developed the ability to accept a compliment. This is called *belief believing*: believing in the positive *beliefs* of others.

Without an *attitude of gratitude* you won't remember a compliment for very long, but you'll hold onto criticism for a lifetime, often remembering negative comments like, "She said I had a horrible

tip How to Develop an **Attitude of Gratitude**

- Learn to accept compliments: A grateful *thank you* is all that's required.
- Learn to give compliments: One of the best ways to develop confidence is to recognize the good in others.
- Learn to feel pleasure and joy without feeling guilt or having to explain why you don't deserve it.

position and my horse was too fat," years after you first heard it. Something else that makes it difficult to adopt an *attitude of gratitude* is the *"yes, but..." response*: Instead of accepting a compliment you begin your reply with, "Yes, but..." thereby casting doubt on the compliment.

Ride to express, not impress. Ride for a cause, not applause.

An *attitude of gratitude* also allows you to feel proud of your accomplishments without having to announce them to everyone. There's no need to tell the world how successful you are because you already know it. You have no compulsion to justify to others why you act the way you do—why you hack instead of taking a lesson or why you ride bareback instead of under saddle. The choices you make are your own and they just feel right to you.

3 Focus Your Focus

A rider in the middle of an important dressage test notices a spectator beside the arena fanning herself with a stack of paper plates. Frustrated, she looks for her coach to try and send him a message, and even tries to convey her thoughts to the spectator by staring at her with burning eyes. Nothing works: The spectator keeps fanning, and the rider keeps losing her concentration. In the end, she rides poorly, and despite filing a complaint, nothing can be done about it.

The moral of the story is that even though the spectator should know better than to fan herself with a stack of paper plates during someone's dressage test, the rider should have known better than to concentrate on the spectator instead of her test.

Mental Multitasking

Even though many of us may believe we can focus on several things at once, we're not nearly as good at *multitasking* as we think. Studies have shown that fewer than 3 percent of us can multitask. People who can are called "super-taskers." The real problem is that most riders think they're super-taskers, even though there's a really big chance (97 percent!) that they're not.

Our brains are wired for something called *selective attention*—we can really only focus on one thing at a time, so we must select what we pay attention to. This means that if you want to fully focus on your dressage test or a jump course, you must avoid focusing on other things, like past mistakes, your competitors, or the crowd. Even momentarily shifting your attention from your ride can cause you to underperform.

This is called *shift tasking* or *"inattentional" blindness* because you're no longer able to fully focus on your ride (you become blinded) because you're shifting your attention between too many things. Texting while driving is a good example. You may be great at texting and great at driving, but do them together and your skill in both will likely drop dramatically. The same thing happens when you try to

No texting and talking while riding!

Pay attention to what you are paying attention to.

ride a dressage test while thinking of the judge, or ride a jump course while thinking of the standings.

Internal Concentration and External Focus

Different riding disciplines require different kinds of concentration. A *narrow* beam of *external focus* may be best to identify the distance to a jump while a *broad* beam of *internal concentration* might be best suited for feeling transitions in the dressage arena. There's also a big difference between the kind of concentration required for training or showing. For example, when learning to jump, it's best to use a *narrow, internal concentration* to focus on what your body is doing and feeling, but when it comes to showing, it's best to use a *broader, external focus* so that you can see the big picture of how each jump will come together to form the complete course.

I'll discuss many different concentration-building exercises in this book, but each of them will work in the same basic way. You'll begin practicing them in a calm and quiet location, and once you're able to concentrate for a full minute, you'll increase the

Concentration

Concentration works like a flashlight: When you shine it in the right direction it can be very helpful; when you shine it in the wrong direction (toward spectators, for example) it won't be of much help. When the beam is focused narrowly on the few important aspects of your ride it can be helpful but when focused too widely (on too many things at once), it can be harmful. A flashlight can also shine *internally* (inside your body to identify things like rhythm and breathing), or *externally* (onto aspects of your ride like the approach to a fence or the height of a jump). When your *focus flashlight* (concentration) is turned off, you'll just find yourself in the dark.

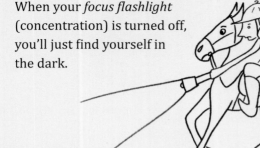

challenge by doing them in a distracting location—beside a TV or while listening to music, for example. Once you can do this you increase the challenge again by attempting it surrounded by a large group of people engaged in a loud conversation. When you can maintain your concentration in situations like these you can maintain your concentration anywhere.

Don't hesitate to motivate!

4 Maintain Motivation

Motivation is what makes you want to get up instead of give up, jump up instead of fall down. It's what makes all the hard work possible and worthwhile. There are many different types of motivation including *inter-*

When Bad Things Happen to Good Riders

A jumper confidently begins her course by jumping her first six fences wonderfully well. Everything is going great: She feels fantastic, her form is excellent, her horse is comfortable, and she notices the crowd is really enjoying her ride. Then, all of a sudden, she knocks Fence 7 to the ground, which causes her to get tight and frustrated. As a result, Fence 8 comes down, too. Dwelling on her mistakes, she loses her focus, which causes her to miss a change, lose a stirrup, and get left behind over Fences 9 and 10. Rushing to get back into shape, she chips into Fence 11 and pulls her last fence.

Question: When did it start to go wrong? Was it when she pulled Fence 7? Maybe when she got frustrated? See below for the answer.

Answer: It started going wrong when she noticed the crowd was enjoying her ride. If she'd been completely focused, she wouldn't have even noticed the crowd. Since she did, she proved that she was not totally immersed in the moment.

nal drives—motivation that comes from within—and *external incentives*—motivation that comes from your environment. In order for you to feel highly motivated, you need a great deal of *internal drive* and/or *external incentives.* Ideally, you'll have plenty of both.

Internal Drives and External Incentives

Internal drives are the personal desires and emotions that compel you toward your goals: Improved self-esteem and a love of riding are two good examples. *External incentives*, on the other hand, are factors that motivate you from the outside, such as moving up a level, earning an instructor's certificate, or even winning ribbons. Drives and incentives usually need to work together: When one is weak, the other needs to be strong, or else you might lack the motivation needed to push toward your goals.

Motivation isn't about what you get. It's about what you give.

Reward Is Not a Motivator

We're often *rewarded* for being *motivated,* but you must use caution when using *reward* as a *motivator*. Internal drives tend to be much stronger predictors of success than external incentives. For example, a rider with a *real* desire to learn to jump will likely do much better than a rider who wants to jump just because everybody else is, or because she wants to win a blue ribbon.

Another reason you should avoid using reward as a motivator is because reward can unintentionally shift your motivation from your riding to the *incentive*. For example, if someone who loves riding is given a ribbon each time she rides well, her reason for riding may change from the love of the sport (*internal drive*) to the ribbon (*external incentive*). In the end, she might even lose sight of her original love of riding because she's become more motivated by a small piece of colored ribbon than by riding her horse.

As I discussed earlier on pages 10 and 11, there are two additional types of motivation. *Fear-driven* is the kind that drives you to avoid things that make you uncomfortable; *success-driven* is the kind that drives you to accomplish things you know you're capable of achieving. Even if you're not able to accomplish it today you know you'll be able to accomplish it soon. In this way, it becomes obvious that courage and patience play a big role in motivation. *Success-driven* riders have the courage to drive for success and the patience to wait for it. Doors open for these riders but remain firmly closed for those who are motivated by *fear* or *external incentives* alone.

There are many causes of low motivation, including excessive pressure and stress, unreasonable expectations, a lack of previous success, and too much perceived possibility of failure. Luckily, there are just as many ways to improve your motivation.

5 Maintain Mental Toughness

Mental toughness is the difference between courage and discouragement; going for it or quitting; self-belief or excuse-making. It's what makes you shift into another gear when you face a challenge, and it's what makes you say things like, "Go hard or go home!"

How to Improve **Your Motivation**

- Recall positive memories of past successes.
- Set exciting goals that keep you engaged and positive.
- Work with a riding mate to keep each other motivated.
- Make a list of what drives and motivates you (e.g. moving up a level).
- Make an effort to create more fun and enjoyment in your riding.
- Visualize success (*imagining* being motivated can cause you to *become* motivated).

The Challenge Response

Choose persistence over resistance.

Being mentally tough means you are not afraid of taking risks, making mistakes, or facing challenges. This is called the *challenge response,* and it often dictates just how successful and *Pressure Proof* you'll become. In the face of a challenge you have the choice to become engaged, focused, and confident, or to doubt yourself, run from the challenge, and quit. You can embrace what's hard and run toward it, or you can turn around and run away from it. The more confident, responsive, and resilient you become, the greater chance you'll have of riding to your full potential. In sports, this is often called a "fighting spirit."

Mental toughness isn't hereditary but it can be learned: If you don't have it, you just haven't learned it yet. The first step to developing a fighting spirit is to avoid panicking when things get crazy; remain calm when tempers flare; stay positive after making mistakes; and never give up when things get challenging.

Even humor can play a role in toughness: Instead of feeling embarrassed after a fall, you can say to those who witnessed it, "Would you mind calling 911 now because I think I'm going to need them sooner or later!" Mental toughness is about finding the spirit to fight on regardless of the challenge; a little self-esteem, self-confidence, and self-belief is all that's needed.

Signs of Mental Toughness

- **Emotional Flexibility**—The ability to absorb an unexpected emotional turn of event and to remain focused and positive in spite of it.

> "We choose to go to the moon...and do the other things, not because they are easy, but because they are hard."
> — John F. Kennedy

- **Emotional Responsiveness**—The ability to remain emotionally alive, engaged, and connected under pressure.

- **Emotional Strength**—The ability to exert confidence and a fighting spirit despite the odds.

- **Emotional Resiliency**—The ability to take an emotional punch and bounce back quickly from disappointment, mistakes, and missed opportunities.

Go out on a limb. That's where all the fruit is!

Mottos like, "When the going gets tough, the tough get going," and "It's not the size of the dog in the fight, but the size of the fight in the dog," are often used to describe mental toughness. It can also be described as "feeling up to the challenge," being energized, alert, and always ready for anything. In a sport as fast-paced and challenging as ours, *mental* toughness might just be more important than *physical* toughness when it comes to becoming *Pressure Proof*.

6 Remain Focused on Solutions

There are two ways to look at every challenge: you can focus on the *problem* or you can focus on the *solution*. When you constantly focus on the problem, called a *problem-focused mindset,* you only see the negative and struggle to find a solution because you're not even looking for it. You become so blinded by the problem that you can't see the solution.

Never hold on to what's holding you back.

The opposite is the *solution-focused mindset,* where rather than dwelling on the problem, you look for solutions and become so "blinded" by the solution that you can no longer see the problem. Instead of feeling bad about starting so poorly, you fight to finish strong; instead of feeling bad about a poor dressage score, you use the judge's comments to

improve; and instead of getting frustrated after pulling a rail, you identify why it happened so you can lessen the chance of it happening again in the future.

It takes very little effort to identify a *problem* but a lot to rise above it and identify the solution. This is why so many riders play the *"I don't know" game.* When asked, "What's wrong?" "What happened?" or "What can I do to help?" many riders simply answer, "I don't know," which proves that they're not looking for a solution but only thinking about the problem.

Positive things happen to positive people.

Two ways to stop playing this game are: (1) refusing to answer any question with "I don't know," and (2) delaying your answers so you can find a solution. When it comes to the *"I don't know" game, haste* makes *waste* but *wait* makes *great.* Instead of saying the solution didn't cross your mind, wait a few seconds so that it can!

The Positive Perspective

A boy is hitting a baseball in the backyard. Three times he throws the ball in the air and three times he swings and misses: strike three. His mom asks (focusing on the negative), "Does that make you sad?" He replies (focusing on the positive), "No I don't feel sad, it actually makes me happy because it proves that I've become a great pitcher!" Riding is much like this; it's all about the positive perspective.

Many problems have similar characteristics: They're often *out of your control* (like when your trailer breaks down or your horse pulls a shoe before a class), or they're *based on the thoughts of others* (when you're being judged during dressage or when you try and live up to the expectations of others). Since you have little or no control over either, it makes a great deal more sense to focus on the solution rather than the problem.

> **tip**
>
> ## How to Become **Solution-Focused**
>
> - Always remember there's a solution to every problem; if you believe it you'll never give up looking for it.
> - The *solution-focused* mindset is contagious so surround yourself with riding mates who are great problem-solvers.
> - Become a role model by teaching others to be positive. It's one of the best ways of becoming positive yourself.
> - Always have a predetermined solution ready (a *motivating motto*, for example, p. 128) so that the next time you encounter a problem you'll know where to start.
> - Remember to be a problem-solver by asking, "What's the one thing I can do to make this better?"
> - Change negative self-questions from *"Why"* ("Why does this always happen to me?") to *"What"* ("What must I do to overcome it?").

Another issue is that many of us tend to take the positive for granted. Rarely do we hear someone who spilled ketchup on their britches yell, "Yeah, 98 percent of my britches aren't covered in ketchup!" or hear a rider who fell off yell, "Yeah, I stayed on longer than I thought I could!" Even though we experience an average of three times more positive events than negative ones each day, the ones that we often dwell on seem to be the negative.

The doors of opportunity are marked "push."

7 **Learn to Trust**

One of the greatest differences between good riders and great riders is that the great ones are able to compete as well as they train the horse. They've found the solution to overcoming the tension, nerves, distractions, and pressure, and it allows them to replicate their practice skills when it really counts. The many tools discussed in this book will help you to do this, but beforehand, you must first learn two more mindsets that lead to becoming *Pressure Proof*.

Schooling and Showing Mindsets

The *schooling mindset* is the attitude with which you learn new technical, mechanical, and mental skills when you practice. To do this you can allow yourself to be a little self-critical, self-judging, and analytical because this is how learning often takes place (you analyze how well you performed a skill in your lesson and judge your performance based on that).

The second mindset is called the *showing mindset* and unlike the *schooling mindset,* it has a relatively easy job to do. Instead of learning new skills through constant self-critique and analysis, all it has to do is believe in your ability and *trust* that the skills you've learned in your practices will be enough.

Live riding as an exclamation not an explanation.

Sadly, this isn't always as easy as it sounds because many riders tend to have a stronger *schooling mindset* than *showing mindset*, which makes it hard for them to trust that the skills they've learned will be enough. As a result many riders freeze or choke under pressure, not because their showing skills are inferior to their schooling skills but because they're trying to show with the analytical and critical *schooling mindset*. In sports this is often referred to as *paralysis by overanalysis*.

Developing good riding habits, mechanics, and technique in your lessons is important, and when your *schooling mindset* is strong, these skills become natural and automatic. This is called *muscle memory* and is the Holy Grail of athletic success. It's this *muscle memory* that you must learn to trust when it comes to showing. Plenty of repetition, analysis, feedback, and time are required to create *muscle memory*.

Constructive criticism **becomes** *destructive criticism* **when you take it from the schooling arena to the show arena.**

In addition, a strong *schooling mindset* can help you build *mental memory* as well. Developing emotional skills like confidence, self-belief, and motivation in your lessons (to the point where they become automatic) is just as important as creating automatic and natural physical skills. One easy way to do this is called *simulation training*: making your schooling sessions feel like a show. This is why basketball teams scrimmage during their practices—they take the good habits, mechanics, and techniques learned in their lessons, and test them by making the practice feel like a real game. By adding a little pressure to your schooling sessions you can start to develop the automatic confidence, motivation, and focus that's so important to showing well.

Showing = showing off what you've learned in your lessons.

The *showing mindset* is a subconscious skill that helps you avoid over-thinking, overreacting, and overanalyzing during competition. The time for all that has passed; the time for self-analysis and criticism is gone; and the time for *trust* has arrived. Studies have shown that no appreciable learning of a skill—mechanical or technical—takes place on show day. This only happens at home during your lessons. So trying to improve while showing is an ineffective use of your time. As soon as you drive into the venue's parking lot or exit the warm-up arena, you need to confidently transition from your *schooling mindset,* to your *showing mindset,* and just *trust* that all the self-critiques, analysis, and feedback from your lessons have prepared you well for the demands of the next few minutes.

Showing with a *schooling mindset* also creates the impression that the harder you try, the harder it gets. For example, the more a jumper tries to see the distance to her next fence the harder it becomes (the dreaded "deer-in-the-headlights" syndrome), and the harder a dressage rider tries to sit up perfectly straight, the more tense she becomes.

Luck vs. Effort

Blindfold a rider, give her a handful of horseshoes to throw, and sooner or later she'll hit the target—not because she's gifted but because she got lucky. Take the blindfold off and give her some lessons, and she'll hit the target much more often—not because she's lucky but because she's taken the time and put in the effort to develop her skills.

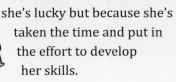
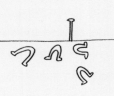

How to Develop a **Strong Showing Mindset**

- **Try "Softer"**—Trying too hard or schooling when you should be showing can lead to pressure and fear of failure. Replace anxiety and self-criticism with self-belief and confidence.
- **Focus on a Task**—Focus on a positive task, like repeating the motto, "Trust not train," to stop your *schooling mindset* from getting in the way of your showing success.
- **Use a "Show-Starter"**—Identify a cue that will create a *boundary* between your *schooling* and *showing mindsets*. For example, tell yourself to "start" your *showing mindset* when you hear the ding of the bell before your dressage test or when you walk into the start box before going cross-country. The sound of the bell, and the location of the start box, sets the boundary between your mindsets.

When you show, no matter the discipline, it just happens too fast; you don't have the time to analyze the height of your hands, the placement of your leg, or the position of your hips. You must turn off your conscious thoughts and allow your subconscious to take over. You're on *autopilot,* trusting your training, and just letting it happen. In riding, this is often called *riding freely,* and it is here that you learn to *trust,* not *train*.

In order to ride well and compete at your best you need to develop a strong *schooling* and a strong *showing mindset*. This means that your mental approach to showing must be very different than your mental approach to schooling.

8 Stay Focused on the Present

Let the past go past.

Staying grounded in the present moment—focusing on the current transition, jump, stride, or movement—is a sure way to increase your chances of riding to your full potential. Called the *present-moment mindset*, it's what ensures you stay focused on doing what's needed to succeed in the *present*, rather than reliving *past* mistakes or hoping for *future* results.

One thing that can make the *present-moment mindset* difficult is a result-oriented lifestyle. We work hard in school *now* so that we'll get into a good college in the *future;* we train horses well *now* so they'll fetch a higher price later; and we work day and night as a working student now to get the chance of riding a great horse in the *future*.

Make peace with your past so that it doesn't ruin your present.

To ride your best you must stay *focused on the best* (yourself in the present moment) and *forget the rest* (other people and other times). An interesting way to do this (in addition to the techniques I'll describe later in this book) is to treat your riding as if it were a dressage test—that is, checking one small box at a time before going on to the next one.

The opposite of the *present-moment mindset* is the *future-focused mindset*. Focusing on potential future standings or outcomes can cause you to become distracted and rob you of the focus needed to ride well in the present (which actually decreases the chance of achieving the outcome you desire).

> It's not where you've gone but where you're going. It's not what you've done, but what you're doing.

The *future-focused mindset* also causes many riders to consider giving up or quitting. Focusing on outcomes that are far in the future can leave a rider feeling overwhelmed and that the time needed to achieve the goal isn't worth the effort. For example, if you tell a rider to quit smoking for the rest of her life she might struggle with the enormity of the decision and decide to not even try (even if she believes it's a good idea). Tell her to quit smoking for today only, and she'll likely feel more capable of accomplishing it (tomorrow you can tell her to quit for *today* again, and so on). In this way, one day at a time, she's more likely to feel less overwhelmed by the challenge and, therefore, feel more capable of achieving it.

9 Peak Your Arousal

Being in the correct state of arousal isn't really a feeling or emotion but rather a range of physical and mental readiness that ensures you're prepared to ride your best. When riders are lethargic, bored, and unmotivated they'll *underperform;* or when anxious and jittery, *overperform.* Some need to get pumped up while others need to calm down. Some like to be alone while others need to be in a crowd, and some arrive early while others get there at the last second.

Yesterday is history. Tomorrow's a mystery. Focus on today.

In order for you to become *Pressure Proof,* you need to find out who you are as a mental athlete, and to do this you need to identify something called your *individual zone of optimal functioning (IZOF).*

APATHETIC: under-motivated
AROUSED: motivated
→ ANXIOUS: over-motivated

Individual Zone of Optimal Functioning

One way to find your *IZOF* is to think of three simple words: *apathy, anxiety,* and *arousal.* When you ride in an *apathetic* way your mind wanders and motivation drops. This is called being *under-motivated.* Ride in an *anxious* way and you'll become worried, tense, and preoccupied. This is being *over-motivated.* Ride feeling *aroused,* however—in your *IZOF*—and you'll feel energized, excited, and engaged. This is simply called being *motivated.*

Another way to find your *IZOF* is to remember that *ideal arousal* feels like a good case of the *butterflies*—that is, filled with positive anticipation that makes it possible for you to ride with vivacity and excitement. On the other hand, feeling *too much arousal* can feel like *horseflies* churning in your stomach—you feel worried, full of doubt, and hesitant. Finally, *too little arousal* feels like almost imperceptible *fruit flies* in your stomach—you feel lethargic, bored, and unmotivated.

Confident riders feel butterflies. Nervous riders feel horseflies.

When identifying your *individual zone of optimal functioning* you should take into consideration several things, including:

- **Your Nature**—If you're naturally tense you may need to calm down; if naturally lethargic, you may need to pump things up.

- **Your Riding Discipline**—The kind of arousal needed for barrel racing or pole bending is quite different from what is needed to succeed at dressage.

- **The Situation**—A jumper may decide to ride calmly in the beginning but pick up intensity toward the end to ensure she doesn't incur time faults.

- **Your Horse**—This is unique to riding (as if it wasn't hard enough already). If your horse is naturally tense you need to ride calmly; if he's naturally lazy, you need to ride energized.

10 Ride in the Zone

When you ride with all the qualities discussed in this chapter, you arrive at a place where everything just seems to go well and feels natural and automatic. You've become *Pressure Proof*. These qualities include:

- Self-Confidence
- Positive Self-Image
- Concentration
- Motivation

How to Find **Your IZOF**

- Create purposeful *actions* that create the level of arousal you're looking for. For example, when feeling rushed, calm yourself down by purposely walking and talking slowly. When you're feeling bored or lethargic, pump yourself up by jumping up and down and shaking your shoulders vigorously. This is called *action-reaction*: These *actions* create the *reactions* you're looking for.

- Take a few deep breaths. Stress causes your heart rate to increase, which, in turn, causes your body's movements to speed up. This is why so many riders rush their courses or collapse their corners when feeling pressure. A few deep breaths can slow your heart rate and, in doing so, also slow the speed of your actions.

- Have a laugh. A good laugh can sometimes help to release the pressure valve so that you can blow off some steam and get yourself back into your IZOF.

- Mental Toughness
- Solution-Focused
- Trust

- Arousal
- Focused on the Present

This place is called the *zone*. You can probably recall a time when your riding felt effortless and automatic, when you were totally immersed in your ride, and everything seemed to happen naturally and fall into place. Likewise, you can also likely recall a time when you felt just the opposite, when everything seemed to fall apart at the seams. You couldn't get into a flow and the harder you tried, the harder it got. The difference between these two rides is that you felt *in the zone* in the first one, but not the second.

There are numerous feelings that characterize the *zone*. Perhaps the most important of all is called the *flow state,* the feeling that everything just seems to flow, falls into place, and takes on a rhythm of its own. You feel as if you're one with your horse and nothing can disrupt it. One challenge with our sport is that many things can rob you of the perception of *flow:* your horse trips a bit, refuses a jump, pulls a rail, misses a change, spooks at a butterfly, or lets out a happy buck. All these can happen in the blink of an eye, and every one of them can interrupt your feeling of *flow*, thereby robbing you of your ability to ride *in the zone*. Luckily, there are many other characteristics of the *zone* that you have greater control over.

Go from <u>hoping</u> it'll happen to <u>making</u> it happen.

Ten "In the Zone" Characteristics

1 Total Concentration—The feeling that you're completely and utterly focused on the task at hand. You feel complete freedom from all distractions, including *internal* ones like worry and doubt, and *external* ones like the runaway stallion that just ran in front of you in the middle of the cross-country course.

2 Feeling up to the Challenge—The feeling that you're being challenged but that you have the skills needed to meet that challenge. It's best when the challenge is comparable to your skill level—if it's too easy you'll get bored; too hard and you risk feeling frustrated.

3 Your Action and Awareness Merge—The feeling of being *one* with your horse *and* your actions. It's the sense of *effortless action* that you feel when you're totally absorbed in a task you feel is meaningful.

4 Senses Are Heightened—Your sense of touch, taste, sound, smell, and sight, plus your sense of balance, timing, rhythm, body-awareness, and the sense of doing what's right automatically, become heightened and more intense. You can feel the stitching on the reins, hear a hoof fall from across the arena, and feel complete unity with your horse.

5 Focusing on the Goal—You feel completely aware of what needs to be done to achieve your goal. It's clear in your mind and you're able to use feedback from your ride to ensure you reach it. You know how well you're doing and know exactly what you must do to continue in this way.

Focus your focus to get *in the zone.*

6 Total Feeling of Control—A sense of being able to do anything you want without feeling like you even have to try. You feel in complete control of your mind, body, horse, and your ride.

7 Lack of Self-Consciousness—You find yourself in a wonderful place free of worries, concerns, doubts, expectations, obligations, and fears (regardless of whether it's a fear of failure, embarrassment, letting others down, or even injury).

Use a little less wishbone and a little more backbone.

8 Distortion of Time—You experience the unusual sensation that time either speeds up, or more often, slows down. Sometimes it feels as if time has slowed down so much that you have an enormous amount of time to perform any action even though it may happen in the blink of an eye.

9 The *"Autotelic"* Experience—This is what happens when an experience is so enjoyable that it becomes its own reward. No longer are you concerned about winning or losing—the ride itself is all the reward you need.

10 A State of Flow—A feeling that everything just seems to flow, fall into place, and take on a rhythm of its own. You feel as if you're one with your horse and nothing can disrupt it.

11 Other Pressure Proof Personality Traits

As you can see in this chapter, there's no shortage of positive mental skills that can help you become *Pressure Proof*. In addition to those already mentioned, the following list covers several others that can help you achieve greatness in everything you do.

Accountability—The difference between being demanding of others and being demanding of yourself. Successful riders hold themselves 100 percent responsible for their own success.

Initiative—The difference between *hoping* and *doing*. Successful riders don't sit around waiting for a chance; they create it.

Pessimists find difficulty in every opportunity. Optimists find opportunity in every difficulty.

Passion—The spark (your desire and love of riding) that ignites the flame that pushes you to achieve your riding goals—regardless of how much effort is required.

Commitment—A willingness to sacrifice time, effort, and yourself to achieve meaningful goals that will reach your personal expectations.

Willpower—The ability to see beyond the present and to know that what you do *today* will have a positive effect on your potential *tomorrow*.

Consistency—The knowledge that success is the result of hard work from day to day, week to week, month to month, and year to year.

Optimism—Always remembering that tomorrow is another day. Successful riders refuse to give up and know that an optimistic attitude can help them find solutions and possibilities in the face of the "seemingly" impossible.

Self-Belief—The ability to believe in yourself and your skills, and to have the courage to know that no matter how big the challenge, you're up for it.

Composure—Your ability to stay calm, cool, and collected, avoid panic, and stay focused when things don't go according to plan.

A Letter

Dear Optimist and Pessimist,

While you were arguing about how full or empty the glass of water was, I drank it.

Sincerely,
Opportunist

Resilience—The ability to bounce back, thrive, and mature in the face of adversity, missed opportunities, and mistakes.

Self-Esteem—The degree to which you experience yourself as being capable of coping with challenges and being worthy of success.

I DESERVE THIS.

PRESSURE PROOF PROJECT

Rate Your Positive Mental Traits

Answer the following questions to determine if *positive emotions* can help you improve your riding:

0 = Never   1 = Sometimes   2 = Almost Always

_____ I'm always optimistic, have a positive self-image, and believe in myself.

_____ I remain calm, cool, and composed in the face of adversity.

_____ I'm resilient and bounce back after adversity, missed opportunities, or mistakes.

_____ I embrace challenges rather than trying to avoid them.

_____ I accept compliments and believe in them.

_____ I have great concentration and remain focused on a task for as long as needed.

_____ I'm motivated and know what drives me to give 100 percent.

_____ I remain focused on the present, not the future (outcomes, standings, ribbons).

_____ I remain focused on finding solutions rather than dwelling on problems.

_____ I know the difference between my *schooling mindset* and my *showing mindset.*

_____ **Total** (add up your answers).

If your score added up to:

14 to 20
Great—you've learned the value of positive emotions and can use them to ride effectively. There's always room for improvement, so continue to think about what you've read in this chapter.

8 to 13
You're on the right track but need more training to improve your riding emotions. Make a list of the challenges that bother you the most and start improving them using the tools in this chapter.

0 to 7
You tend to focus on negative emotions and need a mental-training program to improve. Read this chapter again, and the next one, and make a plan to help change your negative emotions to positive ones.

4

Negative Mental Traits

"Life is not measured by the number of breaths we take, but by the moments that take our breath away."
—Maya Angelou

There's No <u>Right</u> Way to Do the <u>Wrong</u> Thing

If you ride long enough you'll surely encounter some kind of mental challenge. It could come in the form of pressure, rushing, show jitters, other people's expectations, or distractions, and these could make you doubt your ability, lose confidence, make an error, or choke. These are called *destructive emotions* because they rob you of your ability to ride to your full potential. The weight of the challenge can weigh you down, or you can rise up above it. Getting weighed down is easy (that can happen to anyone), but rising up is often hard. It takes thought, effort, and training to overcome destructive emotions, but with a little hard work, it's entirely possible. The purpose of this chapter is to identify the many common types of destructive emotions that can interfere with your ability to become *Pressure Proof*.

Pressure Proof **Your Potential**

1 **Stress**

Stress is a general term used to describe feelings such as anxiety, tension, and pressure. It has many common signs including frequent mood swings, being easily frustrated or annoyed, irritability, impatience, and overre-acting to even the smallest of things. Trouble concentrating, difficulty making decisions, feeling less pleasure than normal, and finding simple tasks a burden, are other signs that stress may be getting to you. In order to completely understand how stress affects you, it helps to know the different kinds:

Time-Limited Stress—Stress that starts early, lingers, and then ends once the stressful situation has been completed—for exam-ple, competing in front of a judge or galloping a cross-country course.

Meaningful Stress—Stress that's somewhat positive because there's a potential for gaining something important—for example, a job interview for a working-student position, or writing an instructor-certification test.

Perceived Stress—Stress that doesn't exist now, but may occur in the future. It can still be stressful worrying about something that might happen soon—for example, anxiety about moving up a level next year.

Destructive Emotions

Stress	Anger
Fear of Failure	Loss of Confidence
Performance Anxiety	Choking
Perfectionism	Loss of Focus
Dwelling on Mistakes	

Background Stress—These are all the daily hassles that seem small but can really add up in the end: a water truck spooking your horse or a misplaced helmet before an important competition.

Other forms of stress can be even more destructive. They include *chronic stress,* like having to alter your life for a long period of time such as caring for a horse after a major injury; *distant stress,* like a bad fall in your past that still affects you today; and *event-sequence stress,* like needing to find a horse to buy after outgrowing a pony.

Don't major in minor things.

Coping with Stress

Stress can have the rather unusual habit of speeding things up: When feeling stress you often feel as if you're on a runaway train that's threatening to jump the tracks. It causes your brain to release adrenaline that makes you rush your thoughts, skip important decisions, and feel like you're out of control.

Learning to overcome stress means learning to slow things down by using deep breathing, relaxation techniques, a calm memory recalled from your past, or even singing a few lines from a calm song. Acting calm by walking and talking slowly, or creating a predictable pre-competition routine, can also help stop the rush before it arrives.

Cope Don't Mope!

When it comes to dealing with stress you can either *cope* or *mope.* You *cope* by focusing your efforts on changing what you can and making peace with what you can't, and by identifying and eliminating the source of the problem using the tools described later in this book. You *mope* when you allow yourself to feel upset, frustrated, helpless, and

After a fall, don't get *upset*—just get *up*!

Kinds of Coping Mechanisms

Anticipatory—Learn to prepare for a future stressor by mentally reviewing how you coped with a similar one in your past.

Problem-Focused—Identify a stressor and then purposely confront it head on (if crowds stress you out, seek out large groups of people to ride in front of).

Emotion-Focused—Consciously change the way you feel about a stressor (if judges stress you out, tell yourself, "I learn the most from constructive criticism").

full of doubt. For instance, after a fall you can *mope* by getting upset and frustrated, or you can *cope* by getting right back on and learning from it.

2 Fear of Failure

Trying and failing is always better than failing to try.

Perhaps one of the most destructive of all emotions is *fear of failure*. This is not your normal everyday fear of being injured; it's the fear of making a mistake, letting others down, embarrassing yourself, being judged, not riding to your potential, looking worse than others, or proving that all your hard work has been for nothing. It's been said that up to 80 percent of all riders and athletes experience *fear of failure* at some point in their careers. What makes it really interesting is that we were only born with two fears: the fear of falling and the fear of loud noises. All the others, including the *fear of failure*, we've learned.

> A diamond is an ordinary hunk of coal that becomes extraordinary under pressure. You can become crushed under the weight of pressure, or you can become extraordinary, like a diamond.

Causes

Worrying about what might happen in the future can easily result in a *fear of failure.* This means that the root problem is the *future-focused mindset;* if you can avoid focusing on future consequences by staying in the *present-moment mindset* you can avoid much of this fear. Infants prove it all the time: Even though they deal with failure on a daily basis they don't develop a *fear of failure* until much later in life (after they've learned to walk and talk) because they never think of the consequences of letting others down, or of not living up to the expectations of someone else. They simply focus on the task at hand and keep on trying. Perhaps we should all learn to ride like big babies.

> "I'd rather fail at something I love than succeed at something I hate."
>
> — George Burns

Social approval is another major cause of *fear of failure.* It includes worrying about what other people think and trying to live up to their expectations or being afraid of letting them down. A need to earn respect or validate that you deserve praise is usually the culprit. To stop this way of thinking, avoid seeking confirmation from others and just learn to ride for your horse and yourself. You can't do this if you're constantly trying to impress your coaches, parents, and other riders, especially if you keep looking over your shoulder at them every time you make a mistake to see if they noticed it.

Fear of failure can also occur when you're in the position of being judged by others. This is why many event riders struggle with the dressage phase more than the cross-country (even though jumping cross-country fences at several hundred meters per minute is inherently more risky than performing a dressage

Fear of Success

Believe it or not, some riders can actually create a *fear of success.* It happens when a rider thinks something like, "If I do well now, people will expect me to do well in the future, also." In this case, a *fear of failure* has been replaced with a *fear of success.* The root cause, however, is still the *future-focused mindset.*

test). It's not the *physical* fear that gets them into trouble; it's the fear of being judged that really trips them up.

Fear of failure can also be caused by a rider's own expectations. For example, the rider who continually begs her trainer to let her move up to the next level is confident of her ability *until* she all of a sudden realizes that everyone expects her to be able to do it. Now the pressure really hits because of the possibility of not being able to live up to her own expectations.

It's been said that Thomas Edison attempted to invent the light bulb over 10,000 times and failed on every single attempt except the last one. When asked about it, he said, "I didn't fail at all; I successfully found thousands of ways how *not* to make a light bulb," proving that we don't need to fear failure, but instead embrace it as a part of learning.

Great athletes prove it every day. Michael Jordan, one of history's most prolific athletes, has been quoted saying, "I missed more than 9,000 shots in my career, I lost 300 games, and 26 times I was trusted to take the game-winning shot and missed. I've failed over and over again in my life,

**FEAR is:
Forget
Everything
And Run. Or,
FEAR is Face
Everything
And Ride.
The choice is
yours.**

Fail Your Way to Success

Failure is a daily occurrence in sports. A major-league baseball player can get paid millions of dollars even though he swings and misses 66 percent of the time. A basketball player can win a major championship and miss 25 percent of his free throws. And a tennis player can win Wimbledon with 30 unforced errors hit into the net. All these athletes have learned that in order to succeed they must accept failure from time to time.

but that's why I succeeded." U.S. Olympic wrestler Jeff Blatnick once said, "I learned how to win by learning how to lose—that means not being afraid of losing." There's really no way around it, we learn through failure. Without it, we can't become *Pressure Proof* and we limit how much we learn and how far we can go. Failure either teaches us to swim or causes us to sink.

Riding often works in cycles: Sometimes you ride well and sometimes

Push to Failure

It's been said that if we don't fail enough we haven't tried enough. Perhaps this is why so many new riders are told that they must fall several times before they can call themselves an experienced rider. In athletics, there's an interesting training technique called *push to failure,* and this is how it works: A weight lifter selects a weight so heavy he can only lift it twice but then he confidently tells himself that he's going to lift it three times (even though he knows he'll probably fail). On the third repetition, he gives 120 percent but can only lift it halfway before he fails. He's not discouraged, however, because he knows that if he continues to push his muscles to failure in this way, they'll do two important things—grow and get stronger.

If you ride in the same way—push yourself hard enough to fail from time to time—you'll also grow and get stronger. This is commonly referred to as "pushing to your limits," "pushing to the breaking point," and "pushing outside your comfort zone."

you struggle, but you must always remind yourself easy times will follow hard ones. You just need to be patient through the hard times and remain positive as you wait for things to get better. Patience, perseverance, and self-belief are three of the most important attributes when it comes to overcoming *fear of failure*.

Things will get better; just tell yourself that and never give up. Ships that stop sailing get rusty and planes that stop flying break down—the same happens to us. We don't get the most out of ships and planes by keeping them tied in the harbor or on the ground; we do so by keeping them moving. To get the most out of yourself, you just need to do the same thing—keep moving and never give up.

A fear of failure makes you want to run away from something that isn't chasing you.

Fear of Injury

A *fear of injury* can certainly be considered a negative, but sometimes it can actually be a positive when used in the right way. There are two kinds of fears: *irrational* fears like a fear of making mistakes or letting someone down, and *rational* fears like being scared by a spooky horse.

All it takes is a good fall to know where you stand.

This second kind is considered *rational* because, in a way, it can help protect you from harm. For example, if a horse spooks every time he passes a pile of poles, you might decide to stop going to that part of the arena for a while. You've now developed a small fear of the poles in the corner, but it could be considered a *rational* fear if it helps you avoid a situation that could jeopardize your safety. Once you recognize the fear, you can start to *desensitize* yourself by replacing the poles with a big bag of carrots. Regardless of the kind of fear, it's always better to overcome it than constantly try to avoid it.

3 Performance Anxiety

Closely related to a fear of failure, *performance anxiety* (or *show jitters*) occurs when you feel apprehensive or unprepared for a challenge such as a show. Together these negative emotions lessen your self-confidence, self-belief, motivation, and ability to ride your best. As a result, you tend to compete in a tentative manner, full of self-doubt.

"During my career I came to bat almost 10,000 times. I struck out about 1,700 times and walked 1,800 times. You figure a ballplayer will average about 500 at bats a season. That means I played seven years without ever hitting the ball."

— Mickey Mantle

Learning to overcome *performance anxiety* means learning to trust your training and focus on the present moment, and on those things that you can *make* happen rather than those that you're afraid *might* happen. You must become 100 percent mentally immersed in your job as a rider so that you won't have any time to focus on feeling anxious.

One thing that can help you accomplish this is a *"honey-don't" list,* a list of things that you *don't* want to think about (standings, expectations of others, and past mistakes, for example). The next time you experience something from your list, remind yourself that it's unimportant and move onto something from your *"honey-do" list*, a list of things you *can* control, like repeating a *motivating motto* or positive *self-image statement* (pp. 128 and 130).

In some ways *performance anxiety* can actually be considered a normal reaction to stress because it proves that you care about doing well. You need to be careful, however, because *performance anxiety* can often be misinterpreted. For example, many riders often mistake something like sweaty palms or a rapid heart rate for anxiety. Instead of welcoming these signs that show they care, they mistake them for signs they are losing control. In this way, it's not really the jitters that create the problem, but the way they are interpreted. Instead of thinking that jitters mean you're succumbing to the pressure, you should learn to believe that it's all just a part of getting pumped-up to ride well—that you're feeling excited, psyched up, and ready to go.

So how can you tell if you are feeling *negative* or *positive* jitters? Well, if they start very early (several days before a show, for example), they're most likely negative. If they start as you drive into the show grounds, they're most likely positive. Likewise, when they linger on and on and don't

> "I'd rather attempt to do something great and fail than attempt to do nothing and succeed."
> — Robert Schuller

Care less about caring so much of what others think.

Separation Anxiety

seem to go away, they're likely negative. When they go away after a few minutes, they're most likely positive.

4 Perfectionism

Striving for the impossible—that is, *perfection*—is one of the greatest causes of stress and underperformance. It occurs when an intense need to win makes it impossible for you to accept anything less. It makes you tighten up, fret about making mistakes, and focus on standings.

Perfectionists have a constant need for approval and live in a state of anxiety, questioning their judgment; they worry about doing something incorrectly and letting themselves down. They certainly mean well and try hard, but usually overthink, overanalyze—and are self-critical. Instead of measuring their success based on the quality of their rides, they measure it based on the quantity of their ribbons. Sadly, this leaves them with very little time to focus on the many processes that can create the success they desire. They get stuck in the *fear-driven mindset* because they're afraid of disappointment and failure. Often-times, this makes them give up or find excuses not to compete so they can avoid the possibility of being imperfect.

Ride in the pursuit of excellence, not the pursuit of perfection.

On a positive side, *perfectionists* tend to be highly motivated with a very strong work ethic. They're often the first to arrive and the last to leave, work the hardest in lessons, and listen intently to everything their trainer has to say. As a result they're often labeled as *committed* and *hard-working* with a good *schooling mindset*.

While they take pride in these labels they often mistakenly believe that being the best in practice should always make them the best in competition. Setting the "bar of expectation" this high almost always leads to a chain of events characterized by making a mistake, dwelling on it, feeling frustrated because of it, and ultimately becoming disappointed because they've let themselves down. "How could I have made such a stupid mistake? I'm the best student at the barn!" Once this happens, other mistakes commonly follow, all of which create more frustration and more disappointment.

Common Habits of Perfectionists

These riders:

- Place unreasonably high demands on themselves.

- Make mistakes because the fear of underperforming causes them to ride tight and tense.

- Are motivated by ribbons, standings, spectators, and beating their opponents.

- Struggle to ride in the present because they're focused on outcomes.

- Want to win so badly they fear they won't able to live up to their own expectations.

- Attempt to ride with perfect technique, which causes them to ride mechanically.

- Are unable to let go of mistakes, or they make excuses for them.

"Imperfect" written another way is "I'm perfect" (just the way I am).

The difference between the way things are going and the way a perfectionist had hoped they'd go is a common reason for disappointment. This is called *telescopic thinking*: looking at mistakes and failure as if looking through the magnifying end of a telescope so they seem larger than they actually are, but then looking at success through the

"Have no fear of perfection. You'll never achieve it."
— Salvador Dali

other minimizing end so that it looks much smaller than it really is. In the end, *perfectionists* struggle to enjoy success because it was expected; trumped by memories of poor past experiences; not a complete success because it wasn't perfect; or they are already worrying about succeeding in the future.

Perfectionists try to be too good for their own good!

tip   How to Overcome **Perfectionism**

- Set show goals focusing on how you'll *perform*—not how you'll *finish.*
- Learn from your mistakes; they're *learning opportunities* not *missed opportunities.*
- Focus on the solution to a problem instead of the problem itself.
- Focus on yourself, not on others, whether opponents or spectators.
- Recall a moment when you rode well—without being perfect—and act that way.
- Repeat a *motivating motto* (see p. 128) like, "Do your best and forget the rest."
- Stay in the present moment. Avoid thinking of past mistakes or future standings.
- Most importantly, remember that *perfectionism* is no laughing matter but riding is, so always have fun.

5 Dwelling on Mistakes

Mistakes are feedback on how you're doing; they tell you if you need to make a change or just stay on your current heading. Interestingly, successful riders tend to make more mistakes than others because they have the courage and confidence to challenge themselves rather than trying to avoid making mistakes. Instead of dwelling on their mistakes, they con-template, identify the cause, regroup, and find a solution. When they make a mistake it lessens the chance they will make it again, knowing that the more mistakes make, the more feedback they'll receive, and the more suc-cessful they'll ultimately become.

> Little changes make big differences. Improvement doesn't always mean having to get 100% better. Sometimes it just means getting 1% better in 100 different ways.

It's been said that we learn the most from our worst les-sons: Instead of believing that mistakes are *unchangeable* behaviors caused by things out of our control, we should view them as *changeable* behaviors that spark our curiosity and create learn-ing. This is often difficult while showing because our expectations tend to be higher than in lessons; there are more distractions that make it hard to stay focused; and it's more common for us to think of the outcome (meaning we spend more time in the negative, *future-focused* mindset). The pressure of showing can also lead to mistakes being made, which may make us doubt our skill and talent. When all this comes together, dwelling on mistakes interferes with our ability to stay focused and productive.

If the grass is greener on the other side, the water bill is sure to be higher.

Anger is only one letter away from "danger."

 6 Anger

When confronted with a challenge, mistake, or missed opportunity you can either learn from or aggress against it. You can become *furious* or you can become *curious* (i.e. you want to learn from it); *enraged* or *engaged.* The choice is yours.

Feeling *anger* while riding is a rather unusual example of the *fight or flight* response. When faced with a challenge, some riders tend to either *fight* themselves (*anger*), or *flee* from it (*quit*).

"The greatest mistake you can make in life is to continually be afraid you will make one."

— Elbert Hubbard

Kinds of Anger

There are two different forms of anger: The first is *outwardly directed* and is what causes a rider to throw her gloves to the ground or yank her horse's mouth in times of adversity. This is almost always an unintentional response to a challenge—that is, it's not a planned response but a reflex that happens without thinking about it.

The second form of *anger* is *inwardly directed,* and it's much more common. It occurs when we turn against ourselves as things go badly or when we let ourselves down; it is characterized by self-criticism, negative self-talk, and loss of temper. Instead of learning from a mistake we launch a personal attack on ourselves, saying things like, "What's the matter with you?" or "You can't do anything right."

It takes a cool head to stay out of hot water.

This kind of *anger* is also known as *self-directed aggression* or *self-mutiny*: Instead of fighting a single battle against your opponent, you begin a secondary battle against yourself. Sadly, a battle fought on two fronts is much harder to win than one that focuses all its strength in one single direction. Imagine the members of a sports team that fight among themselves: Instead of working together against the opposition, they attack each another. When this happens their chance of success drops dramatically.

Purposes of Anger

Some riders use anger as a sort of "subconscious coping mechanism." Instead of dealing with problems in a confident way a rider uses anger to protect herself from disappointment; to show other people that she's more capable than what they just witnessed; or as a defense mechanism, such as when she says she rode poorly because she lost her temper. Regardless of whether

tip   How to Overcome **Anger**

- Remind yourself that you're all you have. Instead of attacking yourself in response to a challenge, seek out its solution.

- Treat yourself as if you're your own best friend. Would you talk to her like that?

- Learn to love succeeding more than you hate failing.

- Remind yourself that just because you let negative emotions out through anger, it doesn't necessarily mean that you've let them go.

it's *inwardly* or *outwardly* directed, anger is always counterproductive and interferes with your ability to be *Pressure Proof*. Luckily, there are ways to overcome it.

7 Loss of Confidence

When you're confident you feel energized, motivated, up to the task, and focused, but many things can shake your confidence if you let them. Past mistakes, poor outcomes, the reputation of your opponents, and pressure can all contribute to a weakening of your self-belief. *Confidence* comes from things such as recalling past successes (instead of forgetting them); creating positive thoughts; believing in yourself; and focusing on your strengths. If you can develop these skills you can also develop the self-belief needed to improve your *confidence*.

*Challenges should make you **better**, not **bitter**.*

When Bad Things Happen to Good Riders

Jennifer has had incredible success lately. In fact, she's won each of her last five classes. In her sixth class, however, she starts well but makes a silly mistake that causes her to end poorly, eliminating any chance of winning. She gets visibly frustrated and angry, saying things like, "You're horrible," "You're a loser," and "You really blew it this time!"

Question: Would improving her "*self-talk*" solve this situation?

Answer: *While improving self-talk (p. 107) is always a good idea, it probably wouldn't solve this because her verbal attacks were only a side-effect of her inability to handle: (1) making a mistake and (2) being imperfect. If she can learn to ride well and avoid becoming angry in spite of making mistakes (being imperfect), her self-talk most surely will improve.*

Common Causes of Low Confidence

Feeling Doubt—The opposite of *self-confidence* is *doubt*. It occurs when you question your ability and makes you become hesitant and pessimistic, often leading to negative self-talk and *fear of failure*. The main cause of *doubt* is unreasonable expectations: When they're too high you *doubt* your ability to achieve them, or if you set them based on your opponents, you create a win/lose situation that can rattle your confidence. When you can control your expectations, you can usually control *doubt*.

Blowing a Lead—Few things in competition can be as hard to overcome as losing the lead. You worked hard to get in front and it was feeling great for a while, but now it feels like it's all slipping away. This happens because you were focusing on the potential win in the future instead of focusing on the "present processes" that create the win. "Wow, I'm really going to win this!" slowly becomes "I'd better not lose this now," which can become "I can't believe I'm letting this slip away!" All this lowers your confidence and creates the potential for a *fear of failure*.

Getting Caught in a Slump—The feeling that no matter what you do, you just can't seem to get out of a rut can be a reason for questioning your ability. There's no greater example of how your past can hurt your present or future. By focusing on the slump you're not able to focus on the skills that could bring it to an end. You might even try changing your technique, but it doesn't help because you can't fix a *mental* challenge by making a *physical* change. The more you try, the worse it gets, and the worse it gets, the more upset you become, and the more you doubt yourself. Setting achievable goals; focusing on the present; not overthinking things; and trusting that the slump will pass are all ways to bring it to an end.

Never doubt yourself. Even a clock that doesn't work is right twice a day.

Riding Down to the Competition—You work hard to develop good skills only to see them evaporate when you face a competitor who rides at a level far *below* yours. We all tend to perform our best when we feel that our skills are matched by the challenge, so when the challenge doesn't push us, we might not push ourselves. You must, therefore, learn to create your own challenge (one that's more demanding than an opponent), such as jumping a clear round or scoring at least 75 percent in dressage. Challenging yourself in this way enables you to *rise* to the occasion instead of riding *down* to it.

*When **in front** never let up. When **behind**, never **give up**.*

Do your best and forget the rest!

8 Choking

One of the most common challenges in all sports is *choking*. It occurs when the pressure or expectation of a situation causes you to underperform or make costly errors. It leaves you feeling cheated and discouraged because you know you didn't ride as well as you could. All riders are capable of choking—what separates great ones from merely good ones is that they know how to recognize and control choking once it starts.

If you lose your confidence, go looking for it.

While choking may be one of the most upsetting emotional responses to pressure it's not necessarily the most negative. In fact, choking is actually considered more positive than defense mechanisms like *avoidance* or *denial* because it means that at least you care and are emotionally committed to something (instead of quitting or making excuses).

When confronted with pressure your brain releases hormones that can disrupt your focus and positive mindset. This means that choking is more a biochemical response to stress than a sign of weakness. You can learn to control the "choking response" by identifying and eliminating the triggers (such as *expectations* from others, *fear of failure,* or *perfectionism*) that cause it. Another common trigger is the *thought* that you might choke or the *feeling* that you've already begun to choke (the fear of choking may actually be worse than choking itself), so it's important that you also adopt a *solution-focused mindset* instead of a *problem-focused one.*

Why We Choke

In part it's because we think too much. To understand how this can happen it helps to know how our thoughts change as we develop as riders. We can be:

Unconsciously Incompetent—As a beginner rider "you don't know what you don't know!" As a result, your expectations remain pretty low, meaning that pressure, performance anxiety, and disappointment also remain low.

Consciously Incompetent—As you gain experience, you begin to "know what you don't know." This can often be mentally difficult because you know what you want to accomplish but struggle making it happen.

Consciously Competent—As you continue to improve you start to "know what you know" (even though it still requires a conscious effort). This phase often requires hard work but can be quite rewarding.

Unconsciously Competent—After years of hard work you "know what you know" without any thought or effort. Your skills and thoughts become "automatic" during this phase, which makes it possible for you to ride to your peak potential.

An interesting example from the sport of *shooting* (a part of the *pentathlon* that includes show jumping) proves how your thoughts can either cause or control the choking response. An athlete practiced his shooting for five years and averaged 22 out of 25 shots; however, on 25 different occasions he shot 24 straight shots and missed every single last shot. Even though his average accuracy was nearly 90 percent, he went 0 for 25 on the last shot. The likelihood of this happening is 0.000000000000000000000001 or one in a trillion multiplied by ten trillion; in other words—as close to impossible as possible. Yet it happened! When asked about it he said that he started to assume he'd miss his last shots—his thoughts went from *unconscious competence* to *conscious incompetence*. He went on to say, "Each time I reached the last shot I doubted my ability to make it." One day he finally hit his last shot because

Always doubt your doubts.

he focused on relaxing, taking a deep breath, and shooting without over-analyzing or doubting his ability to hit it. Once he did that he returned to being *unconsciously competent* again.

9 Loss of Focus

Your ability to maintain focus on what's important is, well, important. *Pressure Proof* riding requires good focus, and to achieve it you must avoid becoming distracted by the seemingly endless list of things that can rob you of your concentration. Instead of focusing on them you must learn to block them out and concentrate on the many tasks that lead to success. There are several different kinds of focus and each one can help you concentrate and avoid becoming distracted. To help you understand the many kinds, once again think of *focus* as the beam of a flashlight; remember it can be narrow or broad and it can be pointed in any direction (see p. 48).

Attack the problem— not yourself.

Types of Focus

Situational Focus—Shine the *broad* beam of your *focus flashlight* all around you so you can see the *"big picture"* of a situation, then prepare for it and make appropriate decisions. A cross-country rider uses this kind of focus when she walks her course, taking into consideration things such as the topography, surroundings, meter markers, jump locations, and approach angles. The better she's able to focus on these many features, the better chance she'll have of feeling in control of the entire ride.

Selective Focus—Point a *narrow* beam of your *focus flashlight* in the direction of your most important tasks. This is the kind of focus you use when speaking with someone at a noisy party—you concentrate on what they're saying while screening out all other conversations. In riding, you use this kind of focus when you concentrate completely on the jump in front of you while blocking out any distractions caused by the spectators, and when you focus on your dressage test without being distracted by the presence of the judge.

Shifting Focus—Continually change the width and direction of your *focus flashlight's* beam to adapt to the changing demands of your ride. A cross-country rider uses *shifting focus* when she first looks at a fence (narrow focus), shifts her focus to her watch (narrow focus), to her surroundings (wide focus), to a note on her arm (narrow focus), to her landing spot (narrow focus), and finally to the topography leading to the next fence (wide focus).

Memory Focus—Shine the beam of your *focus flashlight* on a memory from your past. You can use this kind of focus to remember the judge's comments from a previous dressage test so you can enact them in the test today, or when you compare your current jump course to one you've encountered in the past. This kind of focus helps you learn from the past and develop strategies.

Learn to focus on performance not placing—self not standings.

Every riding discipline requires a different kind of focus, so it's important that you discover and maintain the kind that's best suited to each specific riding situation and challenge. The average time an untrained mind can remain focused on a specific task can be as short as five seconds; when your dressage test is set to last more than four minutes or your show-jumping round more than 75 seconds, you'd do well to work on improving your focus. Your ability to gain and maintain it (and regain it after unexpected challenges) is one of the keys to riding success.

Go from being <u>stunned</u> to being <u>stunning</u>.

When you're focused under pressure, typical distractions like the weather are nonexistent.

Distractions

Distractions have a negative effect on focus. There are many reasons you might get distracted: dwelling on past mistakes; overanalyzing technique; letting your mind wander during unexpected delays; hearing the cheers from the spectators; focusing on things occurring close by; or letting an opponent "get inside" your head are a few good examples. Distractions can be grouped into one of four different categories:

External—These are the distractions that occur in your environment: for instance, rainy and windy weather; unexpected noises; dogs; water trucks; opponents; spectators; or a runaway horse. These kinds of distractions are out of your control, so your goal shouldn't be to eliminate them but to avoid focusing on them.

We have good intentions in life, but sometimes life gets in the way of our good intentions.

Internal—These occur in your own mind: negative self-talk, doubt, and indecision are a few good examples of the kind of emotions that can distract you. These kinds of distractions are within your control, so your goal should be to eliminate them.

Unrelated—These occur in other parts of your life, they're not related to riding but can interfere with your riding focus. Work or school deadlines; relationship issues; worrying about a big exam; or feeling bad about failing a driver's test are a few examples.

Parking

Immerse yourself in your ride by doing something called "parking." When facing a distraction, "park" it by using a movement cue, such as touching your helmet. When you feel yourself getting distracted, pat your helmet and use that motion as your cue to refocus your focus.

Expectations—An unusual form of distraction, unreasonable expectations can interfere with your ability to concentrate because they force you to focus on future outcomes rather than focusing on what needs to be done in the present moment.

Most distractions are understandably negative, but there are two kinds that are quite positive:

1 Using your horse and riding as a positive distraction from the hassles of your everyday life.

2 Using something like a fun night at the movies the day before a big show to distract you from pre-competition jitters.

Simulation Training

As mentioned before, there are many ways to overcome distractions, including *simulation training.* This is purposely creating a lesson plan that replicates many of the possible distractions that might occur during a show. If noisy spectators distract you, ask several people to make noise during your lessons; if there's a chance you'll need to show in bad weather, plan a lesson on a rainy day; or if crowded warm-up arenas distract you, plan a lesson when you'll have to share the ring with many other riders. Simulating distractions in your lessons is a great way to overcome them in the show ring.

Ride to forget, but never forget to ride.

10 Intimidation

Riding while *intimidated* is never easy because it can cause you to become distracted and doubt your ability. The interesting thing about *intimidation* is that it doesn't always come from your opponents; in fact, the most debilitating form of intimidation comes from within. Unlike *purposeful intimidation* (when a rider sets out to intimidate another), *self-intimidation* occurs when you intimidate yourself by believing your skills are inferior to others'. You can bring it upon yourself by saying things like, "I don't stand a chance because she always beats me." It can also be brought on by focusing on your rankings, dwelling on past mistakes, or even just thinking of the reputation of your opponents.

   Self-intimidation often occurs in the presence of opponents but can also be caused by the presence of spouses, parents, friends, and former

Success comes in "cans." Failure comes in "can'ts."

trainers. For this reason, it's often called the "significant-other" effect: You ride well when you're alone, but struggle to focus when a significant other appears.

There can be many different causes of *self-intimidation* including *perfectionism* (for example, when a rider feels that competing against a strong competitor will decrease her chance of being perfect) and *fear of failure* (for example, when a rider is afraid she'll ride poorly in front of family members). Other causes include:

> "Be yourself. Everyone else is taken."
>
> — Oscar Wilde

- Comparing your skills, talent, success, and experience to other riders' qualities.

- Focusing on the reputation of other riders and their horses.

- Recalling negative past memories that include other riders.

- Thinking of the past, present, or future standing: "They always beat me!"

Being intimidated by others (*purposeful intimidation*) can cause you to doubt your ability, which is a form of *self-intimidation*.

The most common technique to overcome *self-intimidation* is something called *thought substitution*, which is changing your thoughts from "what others might have done" to thoughts of "what you can do." A simple way to do this is to make a list of all your strengths and talents, then remind yourself of this list when you begin to feel intimidated.

What others think of you is none of your business.

Another suggestion is to always focus on the present (what you can do right now to succeed) rather than on the past (what others might have done to you before) or the future (what others might do to you later, like placing in front of you). Here are a few other suggestions:

- Repeat a *motivating motto* like "Do your best and forget the rest."

- Design a *motivating logo* like UP2U (your success is "up to you").

- Recall a *motivating memory* of when you stayed focused and rode well.

- Develop an honest desire to want to compete against the best. It's one of the surest ways to go from being a good rider to a great one!

PRESSURE PROOF PROJECT

Rate Your Abilities

Answer the following questions to determine whether *overcoming challenges* can help you improve your riding:

0 = Never   1 = Sometimes   2 = Almost Always

_____ I always cope and never mope.

_____ I learn from failure rather than fearing it.

_____ I ride for myself (no fear of letting others down or living up to their expectations).

_____ I embrace my imperfections and have no desire to strive for perfectionism.

_____ I accept disappointment without frustration or anger.

_____ I always believe I can achieve; I never doubt myself.

_____ I am motivated and know what drives me to give 100 percent.

_____ I focus on myself and do not allow myself to be intimidated by others.

_____ I always give 100 percent and don't play down to my competition or worry about slumps.

_____ I stay focused and rise above any distractions (external and internal).

_____ **Total** (add up your answers).

If your score added up to:

14 to 20

Great—you've learned the value of overcoming challenges. There's always room for improvement so continue to think about what you've read in this chapter.

8 to 13

You're on the right track but need more training to help you overcome challenges in the future. Make a list of the challenges that bother you the most and improve them by using the tools from this chapter.

0 to 7

You struggle with challenges and need to develop a mental-training program in order to improve. Read this chapter again very carefully, and make a plan to become more confident.

5

Brain Babble

"Whether you believe you can or can't, you are right."
— *Henry Ford*

Are You Thinking What You Think You're Thinking?

Every day you think between 20,000 and 60,000 thoughts, and each one of them has an effect on how you perform: They either motivate you *toward* success or *away* from it. You can't go for longer than about 11 seconds without talking to yourself (that's just how interesting you are!) and up to 90 percent of the thoughts you will have today are copies of those you had yesterday. If you're going to *ride* in a positive way you're going to need to *think* in a positive way.

 Brain babble has been called many things including "internal dialogue," "self-talk," "positive affirmations," and "thoughts." Regardless of the name, your riding *emotions* always influence your riding *motions*: When they're negative, they create *doubt,* and when they're positive, they create *confidence.*

No thoughts are neutral. Even those like "Maybe I can do it," or "I think I'll do well," are still considered negative because they don't deliver their message with 100 percent confidence. The self-fulfilling prophecy, *"Be careful what you wish for, you might just get it,"* describes *brain babble* well. Repeat the words "I can't do it" over and over again and don't be surprised if you get *what you're wishing for*. Every single thought counts so it's important that you learn to use all of them in a positive way.

You can do it—nothing to it.

The Conscious and Subconscious Mind

Let's take a look at how your mind works. When you walk through the barn, do you need to consciously concentrate on every step? When you eat a sandwich must you consciously concentrate on digesting it? Or, when you go to sleep do you have to consciously concentrate on continuing to breathe? The answer is no because your *subconscious* mind takes care of all of these tasks for you. If you had to think of every step, every bite, and every breath you'd never have any time left to ride.

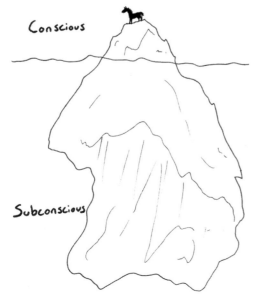

Conscious

Your mind is similar to an iceberg: There's the small part you see—the *conscious*—and the much larger part that you don't see—the *subconscious*. Your *conscious* mind is responsible for making daily decisions, like when to walk through the barn, what to eat, and when to go to bed. It can even help you decide how fast to walk through the barn, how many sandwiches you're going to eat, and what time to set the clock so you don't oversleep. Additionally, it also helps you with basic awareness by telling you that your feet hurt in those boots, that you've eaten too much (sometimes a little too late), and that you're not tired enough to fall asleep yet.

Subconscious

Your *subconscious* mind occupies the much larger portion of your iceberg: The portion that lies under the surface and guides the smaller, conscious portion. Even though you're more aware of your conscious thoughts, it's the hidden subconscious ones that have the greatest impact on your performance because they contain all the programs for moving, riding, talking, solving problems, and more. It's there that all your conscious thoughts get compiled into action. For example, when you learned to canter it took a lot of conscious thought and effort, but with time it became automatic (*subconscious*), therefore no longer requiring the *conscious* effort.

Your mind is like a garden: When you plant a *conscious* thought your *subconscious* will make it grow. When you *consciously* say, "I know my jump course," your *subconscious* mind will work hard to make it happen. It takes what it hears, sets it as a goal then works to make it come true. It believes everything you say to yourself and directs action toward it. You have to be careful, though, because your *subconscious* is not discriminating. It'll grow negative seeds just as quickly as positive ones. This means that if you consciously say to yourself, "I always forget my course," your *subconscious* mind will set it as a goal and work to make it happen as well.

Your *subconscious* mind works by thinking in pictures. If you say to yourself, "I'm confident," it will create a picture of what you look like when

If you say you can, you will. If you say you can't, you won't.

you're confident and then take action to make the picture come to life. Likewise, if you say to yourself, "I'm horrible under pressure," it will create a picture of what you look like when you're not coping well then take action to make the picture come to life. Remember that your subconscious mind always works hard to make your *dominant thoughts* come true.

If you don't have anything nice to say (to yourself), don't say anything at all.

It's also important to remember that your *subconscious* cannot think the opposite of a command. If you say to yourself, "Do not be nervous," it will still paint a mental picture of what you look like when you're nervous. Repeat, "Do not look down," or "Do not be nervous," and the first thing you'll likely do is look down and get nervous. With this in mind, it's important for you to direct your *conscious* thoughts in a positive direction by saying things like, "Look up," or "I am calm," so that your *subconscious* mind gets the picture of you looking up and being calm. Once it's accomplished this, it can set it as a goal and start directing action to make it happen.

Positive Brain Babble

To create positive *brain babble* you must create a positive *cause-and-effect relationship*, which means that your thoughts should *cause* a desired *effect*. You must also create a positive *belief-and-experience relationship*. This means that your *beliefs* should cause a positive *experience* (rather than letting negative beliefs cause a negative experience).

Timing Is Everything

Unlike physical work where fast and hard efforts are rewarded, *brain babble* is often most effective when you're relaxed and calm as you are 15 minutes before falling asleep and immediately after waking. It's during these times that your brain-wave activity slows and puts your mind in a highly suggestive state.

Self-Talk

There are two general kinds of *self-talk*. *Instructional* self-talk like, "Elbows in," or "Shoulders open," work best for fine motor skills like rein aids or for improving your mechanics and technique. *Motivational* self-talk like, "You can do it," or "Stay calm, carry on," are most effective when psyching-up for competition, boosting confidence, improving concentration, or overcoming mental challenges like self-doubt or show jitters.

Your emotions control your motions.

tip How to Create **Positive Brain Babble**

1 Silent Talk—Repeat positive words or phrases in your mind as a way of controlling your thoughts and focusing on the positive. This is the most common form of *self-talk,* and it serves many purposes, including helping you focus on goals rather than fears, and training your mind to think purposely instead of randomly.

2 Hearing Aid—Instead of "thinking" thoughts, say them out loud. This form is considered more powerful than silent self-talk because speaking and hearing your thoughts creates something called a *language loop* by engaging the auditory and verbal portions of your brain, as well as those areas that actually created the thought.

Who's the fairest of them all?

3 Reflection Talk—Verbally repeat a positive phrase while looking at yourself in a mirror. It's best to use a full-length mirror so you can see your body language, and say the positive phrase as many times as possible without looking away. If you can get past the unusual nature of this technique it can have amazing results.

4 Focus Switch—Instead of thinking about what you're afraid of, focus on what you're thankful for. If you're afraid of dressage judges, remind yourself how grateful you are that someone's there to help you identify what you need to work on.

5 Buddy Babble—The words people say to you can have a big impact on your self-image so provide a friend with a positive phrase voiced in the second person like, "You're confident and capable of greatness," or "You're amazing under pressure," and ask her to say it when your confidence is low. Each time she does, reply, "Yes I am, thank you."

Control your thoughts so your thoughts don't control you.

6 Self-Conversation—Verbally engage in a two-sided conversation with yourself. It works best when you ask leading questions and answer them in a productive way. Questions like, "What can I do to get my horse to load?" or "What can I do to make up for an early pulled rail?" encourages you to find good answers to productive questions.

7 Recoded Talk—Listen repeatedly to recorded positive statements. This works best when you listen as often as possible even if you don't always focus completely on them (called *background babble*). You can even add calming or uplifting music to the recordings depending on the message.

Never belittle yourself. Be big!

8 Written Babble—Write down your *brain babble*. It creates the idea that it's more important than random thoughts, increases the amount of time needed to form the thought (so you focus on it for a longer period of time), and helps you to *visualize* your thoughts, especially when you use bold ink, vivid letters, and lots of exclamation points!

Negative Brain Babble

Negative *brain babble* is often called *toxic talk* because it's complaining, argumentative, blaming, and full of self-doubt. It's been said that toxic talk can be up to 35 times stronger than positive *brain babble* (meaning that if you convince yourself you *can't* do something, you may need to repeat "I *can* do it," up to 35 times before you'll start to believe it). For this reason, it's important to avoid thinking negative thoughts in the first place. Here are a few examples of negative thoughts that can easily enter your mind:

- I never remember my test.
- I just always seem to come up short.
- I never get it right.
- You can't teach an old dog a new trick.
- Just my luck.
- I used to be so much better.
- I hate going first.
- I always crumble under pressure.

Focusing on your *weaknesses* ("My position is horrible"), on the *past* ("I can't believe I forgot my test!"), on *others* ("Why did *she* have to show up?"), on the *outcome* ("I must win"), and on *events out of your control* ("I hate riding in the rain") all contribute to creating negative *brain babble*. One way to avoid this is to switch from the *all-about-you* attitude ("I can't believe I pulled the last rail," or "I can't believe I froze up,") to an attitude that reminds you of your horse ("I lost my balance but I love my horse for keeping himself under me.")

You have room for one confident voice in your mind. Make sure it's your own.

There are so many benefits to positive *brain babble* they're hard to count: Changing *negative* self-talk to *positive* helps you increase your motivation; strengthen your confidence; enhance your mood; focus your attention; break bad habits; remain in the moment; cope with adversity; psych yourself up or calm yourself down, all of which lead to improved riding performance and enjoyment. Luckily, there are many tools that can help you create positive *brain babble,* including those that I'll discuss on the next several pages.

Pressure Proof **Your Brain Babble**

1 **Avoid Negative Words**

You can't see the sunrise if you're looking toward the west.

To ensure positive *brain babble* you need to get in the habit of thinking of positive words. The problem is that some negative words disguise themselves as positive. While *typical* negative words like *can't* and *hate* are easy to spot, it's the tricky ones like *think, try, hope,* and *pray* that can really get you into trouble. The reason they're considered tricky is because they actually sound pretty positive; after all, the word *think* indicates a desire to ride with your mind; the word *try* indicates a desire to accomplish something; and the words *hope* and *pray* must be good—after all they're mentioned hundreds of times in the Bible! Use them while riding, however, and you might run into difficulty because the positive thought, "I can do it," becomes "I *think* I can do it," "I'll *try* and do it," "I *hope* I can do it," or "I *pray* I can do it." Sadly, the sentences formed using these tricky negative words lack complete confidence.

Perhaps the trickiest negative word of all is the word *not* because your mind has a very difficult time hearing it. If you repeat the statement, "I'm *not* nervous" a few times quickly, don't be surprised if you start to feel a bit nervous—tell someone who's afraid of heights while standing on a cliff *not* to look down and what's the first thing she'll likely do?

Remember that your *subconscious* cannot think the opposite of a command so instead of telling yourself *what not* to think, tell yourself *what* to think ("I am confident" is better than "I am not nervous"). When you do this, your thoughts deliver their message in a more positive, clear, and understandable way. This is yet another example of the difference between the *problem-focused mindset* ("Don't be nervous") and the *solution-focused mindset* ("I am confident").

Turning negative *brain babble* into positive is easy when you know how. First of all, you should always avoid verbalizing (out loud or to yourself) anything negative about how you're feeling. Telling others that you have a cramp or are too stiff to sit the trot only creates a search for sympathy or a search for an excuse—neither

Pressure Proof Eye Test

Take this simple test to see how easy it can be to think in a negative way. Look quickly at the letters below and identify four words:

ridingisnowhere

Did you come up with riding is "no where," or riding is "now here"?

 tip **Positive** Words

Ready—I'm ready to succeed.
Prepared—I'm well prepared.
Accept—I accept mistakes.
Worthy—I'm worthy of this praise.
Deserve—I deserve to be happy.
Love—I love the challenge.
Comfortable—I'm comfortable riding in front of judges.
Willing—I'm willing to do what it takes.

The "Paper Clip" Technique

This simple technique can help you discover the extent of your negative thinking. Start by placing a pocketful of paper clips in your left pants pocket in the morning, and every time you have a negative thought during the day take one out and put it in your right pocket. Before you go to bed at night count the number of paperclips in your right pocket. Strive to have fewer paperclips in your right pocket the next day.

of them sounding very confident. You should also avoid getting involved with conversations containing gossip, skepticism, or cynicism. Negative self-talk is incredibly contagious so you should stay far away from it. If you must talk about a negative thing from the past (talking with your coach about how show jitters used to bother you, for example), always voice it as if it's long gone rather than an ongoing problem. Using phrases like, "In the past…" or "I used to be…" indicate that the negative habit no long bothers you.

2 Word Substitution

For an interesting and simple way of improving *brain babble*, use *word substitution,* which encourages you to look for—and replace—negative words with more appropriate positive ones. On page 113 I list some negative words and the positive ones you can replace them with.

An example of word substitution would look like this: You start with a negative sentence like, "I don't think I can do it." You improve it by removing the word "don't" so that it becomes, "I think I can do it." You make it better by changing the word "think" to the word "know" so that it becomes, "I know I can do it." The sentence becomes even stronger when you add the word "now" because it becomes, "I know I can do it now." You finalize your positive sentence by changing the word "I" to the word "we" to include your horse. Your new sentence becomes, "I know we can do it now."

If you believe it you can achieve it.

tip   How to Change **Negative Thoughts to Positive Ones**

- Change the word *can't* to the words *love to*. The statement, "I *can't* ride well in front of judges," becomes "I *love to* ride well in front of judges."

- Change the word *hate* to the word *love*. "I *hate* riding first in classes," becomes "I *love* riding first in classes."

- Change the word *think* to the word *can*. "I *think* I can do it," becomes "I *can*, I can do it."

- Change the word *if* to the word *when*. "*If* I ride well today," becomes "*When* I ride well today."

- Change the words *I'll try* with *I will*. "*I'll try* and do it," becomes "*I will* do it."

- Change the word *I* to the word *we*. "*I* can do it," becomes "*We* can do it," and takes into consideration the important relationship with your horse.

- Use the word *now* at the beginning or end of sentences. "I can do it *now*," "I can ride well in front of judges *now*," and "*Now* I can see my distances."

Another interesting example of *word substitution* is when you turn negative *what if* sentences to positive *so what if* sentences. "What if I forget the jump course?" may create self-doubt, but "So what if I forget the jump course?" indicates there'll always be a next time. The pressure just seems to drop when you add the simple word *"so"* to the front of the sentence. While this is certainly a good idea, you can't finish there because the sentence, "So what if I forget the jump course?" can be misinterpreted as not caring or not willing to give 100 percent. You can avoid this by adding a second positive sentence to it such as, "So what if I forget the course? It'll teach me what I need to work on in the future to improve." In this way, you relieve the pressure by adding the word *"so"* to the negative *"what if"* sentence then prove you're willing to give 100 percent or learn from any mistakes by adding the second sentence.

Don't think you can do it. Know you can do it.

If needed, you can even add a third sentence to lighten the mood a bit: "So what if I forget the course? It'll teach me what I need to work on in the future to improve. And besides, I kind of like the courses I come up with anyway!" You've now lowered the pressure; proven you're willing to learn from your mistakes; and, at the same time, are remembering to enjoy yourself.

Pressure Proof Plan **Word Substitution**

Write two common negative words that you think to yourself:

(1) _____

(2) _____

Write a positive alternative for each:

(1) _____

(2) _____

3 **Cue Words**

Perhaps one of the easiest, most creative, and powerful ways to create positive *brain babble* is through the use of a *cue word:* an acronym that reminds you of the important *physical* and *mental* skills that will allow you to ride your best. This simple mnemonic device can help you focus your thoughts in a productive and positive way.

For instance, a jumper who rounds her back and forgets to release should think to herself, "Remember to sit up

Well said is often just as good as well done.

tall, open my shoulders, flatten my back, press my chest forward, relax my arms, follow my horse's movement, and don't forget to release." Unfortunately, in the heat of the moment and under pressure, she probably won't have the time or ability to repeat this massive list. Instead, she can simply summarize it into the simple *cue word* STAR: *Sit Tall And Release*.

Likewise, a rider who overthinks and overanalyzes can use the same *cue word* to remember to *Stop Thinking And Ride*.

Most of us have used acronyms before (RSVP, TBA, 24/7, TGIF, FEI,

BHS, USEF) so it's easy to understand how they can help us manage and remember important things. When creating cue words, it's best if they form short sentences instead of lists because our minds process phrases better than mechanical lists. For example, the cue word "PAT" can describe *Patience, Acceptance, Trust* (try saying that 10 times really fast!) or just *Patience And Trust*. The cue word "BAR" can describe *Breathe, Arousal, Relax* or just *Breathe And Relax*. Whenever possible, you should limit your cue words to five or fewer letters; any more than that and the acronym itself turns into a long list.

Cue Words to Try

As you will see below, *cue words* are just simple acronyms or other mnemonic devices that help remind you of the many things you can do to create success. You know what you must do to ride well, but if you can't remember it, it doesn't help you very much. Without cue words, you can have a pretty difficult time remembering all the great things that'll allow you to ride your best. Here is a list you can use to get started:

Think about what you think about.

SUPER—*Succeed Under Pressure Every Ride*
BIG—*Breathing Is Good*
START—*Stop Thinking And Ride Tall*
BITS—*Balance In The Saddle*
STRONG—*Stay Tough, Ride On, Never Give (up)*
FAITH—*Forget About It, Try Hard*
CREST—*Crest Release Every Single Time*
FAST—*Focus And Sit Tall*

FOCUS—*Find Our Courage Until Success*

PATHS—*Pay Attention To His/Her Stride*

BLAST—*Breathe, Laugh And Smile Today*

LEG—*Let Everything Go; Let Expectations Go; or Let Everyone (else) Go"*

LEGS—*Love Every Good Stride*

BEST—*Balance Every Single Transition*

SMILE—*Smiling Makes It Lots Easier*

LUCKY—*Look Up, Cluck, Kick, (and) Yell!*

UP2U—*It's up to you.*

C ²—*Confident Courage in the corners* (the ² means *squared,* which refers to the two "C"s as well as the corners).

URGR8—*You are great*!

If you are creative with your cue words you might actually be able to bend the five-letter rule a bit. Below are a few examples proving that we're only limited by our imagination. These cue words are actually *cue phrases* containing more than five letters.

SUNSHINE—*Sit Up N' SHINE.*

SHAMROCK—*Straighten Horse And Move, (then) ROCK (on)*!

HEADLINE NEWS—*HEAD up, straight LINE and see the NEW (next) fence.*

Pressure Proof Plan **Cue Words**

Write up to three mental and physical skills you need to remember to ride your best:

(1) _____

(2) _____

(3) _____

Come up with at least one cue word or cue phrase that summarizes each of these skills:

(1) _____

(2) _____

(3) _____

4 Thought Stopping and Thought Replacement

Our conscious minds can only hold one thought at a time (either positive or negative). It's impossible to think we *can't* do something yet believe we *can;* telling ourselves to "stop worrying" doesn't work because we can't concentrate on the opposite of what we're thinking. This means that you must actually choose to think positive thoughts. Remember, you think between 20,000 and 60,000 thoughts a day, and there's no way to stop them happening. This means that you can't make your mind go blank; you must purposely fill it with positive thoughts, or purposely replace negative thoughts with positive ones. Thoughts of worry need to be stopped and replaced with thoughts of self-confidence, and thoughts of doubt need to be stopped and replaced with thoughts of self-belief.

Don't think of what can go <u>wrong</u>. Think of what can go <u>right</u>.

Like with everything else, practice makes perfect so it's important to get in the habit of repeating your *thought stoppers* and *thought replacements* as often as possible. One way to do this is by imagining yourself in a situation that produces a negative thought and then mentally rehearse injecting your *thought stopper* and *replacement*. If possible, repeat them out

tip

How to Stop Negative Thoughts and **Replace with Positive Ones**

1 Thought Identification—One of the first steps to improving self-talk is to recognize the kind of negative words you say to yourself. It's also helpful to recognize the situations that cause you to think these negative words. This will help you anticipate the arrival of *negative brain babble* so that you can form a plan to stop it.

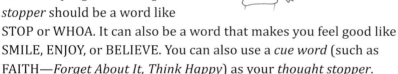

2 Thought Stopping—As soon as you think of something negative, disrupt it by yelling a positive word at yourself. This verbal stop signal or *thought stopper* should be a word like STOP or WHOA. It can also be a word that makes you feel good like SMILE, ENJOY, or BELIEVE. You can also use a *cue word* (such as FAITH—*Forget About It, Think Happy*) as your *thought stopper*.

3 Thought Replacement—After your *thought stopper* has disrupted the flow of your negative thoughts you must be prepared to quickly replace them with more productive, positive ones. To ensure you're able to do this, it helps to have a few positive *thought replacements* handy. They can be a series of pre-selected positive thoughts like, "If it's going to be, it's up to me," or "I believe I can achieve," that you say to yourself once your *thought stopper* has disrupted the negative flow. Without a pre-planned *thought replacement*, your mind will search randomly for its own *thought replacements*, and unfortunately may come up with more negative ones.

loud for the first few times and continue doing it over and over again until it becomes automatic. Once this happens your *thought stopping* and *thought replacement* will stand a much greater chance of helping you in the future.

Pressure Proof Plan **Thought Stopping and Thought Replacement**

Write three *negative* words or phrases that you often think to yourself:

(1) _____

(2) _____

(3) _____

Write one positive alternative for each:

(1) _____

(2) _____

(3) _____

Write your *thought stopper:* _____

_____

Write your positive *thought replacement:* _____

_____

The next time you think in a negative way remember to use your *thought stopper* and *thought replacement*.

5 Question Suggestion

One sure way to create positive *brain babble* is to deliberately ask yourself questions that lead to positive answers. These *leading questions* can have a very positive influence on your thoughts as long as the questions you're asking are positive (questions that point you toward positive answers). In doing so, they help you find the solution to problems instead of only focusing on the problems themselves (a *solution-focused mindset* instead of the *problem-focused mindset*). "What steps can I take to remember my dressage test?" is an example of a positive *leading question* because the answer will help you to formulate a plan of action.

When creating your *question suggestions*, avoid asking yourself negative questions like "Why do I always choke under pressure?" or "Why is everyone better than me?" because they force you to answer the question in a negative way like, "Because I'm weak, I can't handle the pressure, and I'm less talented than everyone else" (negative questions create negative answers). Additionally, these kind of negative questions also *assume* the unwanted condition. For example, if you ask, "Why do I *always* choke under pressure?" you're already assuming you choke under pressure.

It's important that your questions assume greatness instead of weakness like, "How can I make today's ride even better than yesterday's great ride?"

 ## How to Create **Leading Questions**

- Never answer your *leading questions* with the words, "I don't know." The truth is that you probably do know the answers to your hard questions.

- When you say, "I don't know," it only proves that you're unwilling to invest the time and effort to find the hard answers to your hard questions.

- Ask yourself *leading questions* about how you look. For example, "How do I look when I am confident?" Once you create the picture in your mind, change your body language to match it.

- Always answer your questions in a *productive* way so it creates a plan of action. For example, "What must I do to ride well today?" can be answered with, "Think positive thoughts, use my cue word, and balance my corners." Positive question asked and positive question answered (imagine answering the same question with "I don't know").

The answers you get depend on the questions you ask.

- Never answer your positive *leading question* with a negative answer. Imagine replacing the positive answer above with, "Who cares, I'll never ride well anyway." It doesn't help to have a positive question asked but negative question answered.

- Ask "how" questions and avoid "why" questions. "*How* can I jump clean?" creates positive answers, but "*Why* does this always happen to me?" creates negative ones. When it comes to forming a plan it's more important for you to know "how" to do something (like *how* to remain calm) than "why" you do something (like *why* you get nervous).

- Use the general question, "What must I do to ride my best?" to find the answer to any challenge.

- Identify a challenge and ask how to overcome it. For example, ask "How can I relax between classes?" then find three positive answers to help achieve it.

- Ask the question, "What is it about riding I love so much?" Answering this question can only take you in a positive direction.

- After encountering a challenge, offer yourself a "stress debrief" by asking yourself what you learned from it.

- Avoid negative *inflections* in sentences like, "*Why* do I keep doing this?" because it create negative answers such as, "Because I'm no good!" If you must ask questions like this make sure they have a positive inflection so that "Why do I keep doing *this*?" is answered in a positive way: "Because I love challenges."

Leading questions can be great teachers because they encourage you to search out the best answers (they challenge your brain to look for the right response). In this way, it's not really the questions that make the difference but the way you answer them. Perhaps we should judge ourselves more by our answers than by our questions.

Pressure Proof Plan **Question Suggestion**

Write three positive questions:

(1) _____

(2) _____

(3) _____

Write one positive answer for each:

(1) _____

(2) _____

(3) _____

6 "C"ing Is Believing

A common problem with positive thinking is that modesty can sometimes make it difficult for us to compliment ourselves. One trick that can help you say positive things about yourself is to think of the letter "C." In the English language, the letter "C" starts the greatest number of positive riding emotions: You could say to yourself, "I'm so nervous," or you could say, "I'm going to do great because I'm calm, cool, collected, confident, competent, courageous, centered, capable, creative, consistent, careful, caring, coordinated, composed, conscientious, committed, and competitive!"

Open the dictionary and be prepared to be surprised; in addition to those positive "C" emotions you'll also see chocolate, cookies, (chocolate chip cookies!), cakes, candies, coffee, carrots, cupcakes, and more. Take a few seconds and quickly see how many positive words you can come up with that start with the letter "J" or "H." Chances are you might not find as many as those starting with the letter "C."

So just how can the letter "C" help you create positive brain babble? Start by writing down the two positive "C" emotions that describe you when you're at your very best. Are you *confident* and *courageous*? If so, write them down, and *act* that way when you start to feel the pressure rise.

It's normal, however, for some of our confidence and courage to waiver a bit when we experience pressure and stress. If this happens, remind

The ABCs of Positive Thinking

The letter "D" is considered one of the least positive letters in the English language because the "dis" prefix turns many positive words to negative ones. Satisfied becomes dissatisfied; encourage becomes discourage; like becomes dislike; and qualify becomes disqualify.

The letter "I" also starts many negative words because the "in" prefix also turns many positive to negatives. Effective becomes ineffective; correct becomes incorrect; and flexible becomes inflexible. When it comes to riding, you should always feel confident and competent "C" emotions, and ignore the disappointing, discouraging, depressing, dejecting, incompetent, inconsistent, inferior, and insane D and I emotions.

yourself to <u>A</u>lways <u>B</u>e your <u>C</u>s. This is called the ABCs of positive thinking (commonly referred to as *fake it until you make it*). When the pressure of a situation robs you of confidence and courage, *fake* them—by walking, talking, and thinking confidently—until you *make* them. Whatever emotion you want created on the "inside," first create it on the "outside"—that is, *fake* confidence and courage on the outside until you *make* confident and courageous feelings on the inside.

Perhaps the most important "C" attributes are *challenge, change, constructive criticism,* and *control.* When you avoid challenges, change, and constructive criticism, you limit how much you learn and how far you'll go. Overcoming *challenges* proves that you're capable of achieving goals; accepting *change* proves that you can thrive in the face of adversity; and accepting *constructive criticism* proves you're mature enough to learn from your mistakes. The fourth "C" emotion,

Negative brain babble is often caused by a "C" deficiency.

control, is perhaps the most important of all because without it, it's virtually impossible for you to feel confident, competent, content, calm, capable, or any of the other positive "C" emotions.

Pressure Proof Plan **"C" ing is Believing**

Write three positive "C" emotions that describe you:

(1) _____

(2) _____

(3) _____

Write three situations that make you forget your "C" emotions:

(1) _____

(2) _____

(3) _____

The next time you encounter these situations remind yourself to <u>A</u>lways <u>B</u>e (your) <u>C</u>s.

Never let
anyone turn
your sky into
a ceiling.

7 Avoid Trash-Talkers

Emotions are very contagious—both those that are positive and those that are negative. One of the best things you can do is surround yourself with positive people in the hopes that you'll "catch" a little of what they have. Stay away from negative people, and you can *avoid* catching what they have (for example, many people learn to smoke by spending time with smokers). Likewise, many people learn to love riding by hanging around horses and people who love to ride. When emotions are used in a positive way, *contagious* is definitely a positive "C" emotion!

Negative people are often called *trash-talkers* because they dump *verbal garbage* at your feet that can sound something like this, "The footing's horrible because it rained last week; it's so windy the horses are all going to spook; and this judge is so critical I don't even know why we're riding!"

As a rider, you have a choice: You can focus on the negative and bend over and pick up all their verbal garbage by saying, "You're right, the footing might be slick, I didn't realize it was windy, and I didn't know the judge was so mean," or you could focus on the positive and refuse to pick up their garbage by *slamming the lid on their can*. You do this by becoming so overly positive that the *trash-talker* thinks you're a bit crazy (in this case, *crazy* is also a positive "C" word). It would sound something like this, "You're right it did rain last week so it won't be dusty, I love the wind because it keeps me fresh so I won't get sweat marks, and I love critical judges because they remind me of my husband!"

Trash-talkers are everywhere so if you can't avoid them, make sure you avoid picking up their trash. To do this politely, listen to what they have to say, and then quickly turn all their negatives into a positive. When you do this you take the *trash in and turn it around*. Before leaving, however, remind them how wonderful riding is and how lucky they are to be a rider, hoping that perhaps they'll catch some of your contagious positive emotions.

It's hard to expect positive results if you surround yourself with negative riders.

Cancel my subscription. I don't want your issues.

8 Motivating Mottos

Another way to create positive thoughts is to repeat positive phrases, and one sure way to repeat positive phrases is to repeat a positive *motto*. There are no rules when it comes to creating *motivating mottos:* They can be short sentences, song lyrics, catch phrases, or any other form of word play. It can be something well known like, "Just do it"; something private between you and your horse like "241" (the <u>two</u> of us working <u>for</u> <u>one</u> goal); a few lines from your favorite song like, "Be strong and push on," or even a catchy quote like, "Just keep swimming," from the film *Finding Nemo*.

If you can't do everything, just do everything you can.

Once you create your *motivating motto* you need to get in the habit of using it. This can sometimes be difficult because pressure has a strange way of making riders forget important things. When you need it the most, is often when you seem to forget it the fastest. To avoid letting this happen create strategies like making your motto your computer password; repeating it every time you open a door; or writing it on a piece of paper and taping it to your tack trunk. The more you practice and see it, the more it'll become a part of you. Here are a few good examples of *motivating mottos*:

- When in front don't *let* up and when behind don't *give* up.
- If it's going to be, it's up to me.
- Go hard or go home.
- Keep calm and ride on.
- Push on, finish strong.
- Make the impossible possible.
- What doesn't break me makes me stronger.

- If I believe it, I can achieve it.
- We're better together.
- Turn stress to success.
- Do my best, forget the rest.
- Whatever it takes to get whatever I want.

Pressure Proof Plan **Motivating Motto**

Write your motivating motto:

_____

_____

Write three situations where you may need to use it:

(1) _____

(2) _____

(3) _____

Write down three strategies to remember your motto:

(1) _____

(2) _____

(3) _____

9 Self-Image Statement

It's impossible for you to think positive things about your riding if you don't think positive things about yourself. Developing a strong *self-image statement* (a *self-talk* phrase designed to remind you of your strengths) is, therefore, one of the first things you must do. It can help you direct your thoughts in a positive direction; maintain focus under pressure; avoid doubt and distractions; and remind you what you're capable of.

Keep calm and ride on.

The idea behind the *self-image statement* is simple: Knowing what to think usually beats thinking whatever pops into your mind because pressure often has the bad habit of creating self-doubt.

There are two different kinds of *self-image statements*. The first is your *performance statement,* a phrase that reminds you of all the positive *physical* assets you have. The second is your *personality statement*, a similar phrase that reminds you of all your *mental* assets. When used correctly and frequently these positive statements can create a sort of *personal reputation* and you begin to believe what you say and hear about yourself. This is another example of the self-fulfilling prophecy, "Be careful what you wish for—you might just get it!"

When creating a positive *self-image statement*, it's always a good idea to create a *performance* and a *personality statement* for both *schooling* and *showing*. They should be voiced in the present tense and start with words like, "I have," "I am," or "My." Better yet, start

Three Steps to a Positive Self-Image

1 Identify a strength (or strengths) that you have (or want to have).

2 Identify what your strengths could help you accomplish.

3 Combine them into a statement such as "*My great dressage position* will help me *score well* today."

them with, "We have," "We are," or "Our," thereby remembering the important role your horse plays in your riding success. Obviously, your statements should also be voiced in a positive way, so avoid using negative words like "can't," "don't," or "I think." Here are a few good examples:

Performance Statements

Schooling—My balanced seat, stable leg, and supple hips make me a great student.

Showing—My ability to see distances and my balanced jumping position make me supremely competitive.

Dressage—My precise transitions, symmetrical position, and connection with my horse allow us to show our best.

Cross-Country—My balanced approaches, takeoffs and landings, along with the quality of our canter, make us dominant competitors.

Personality Statements

Schooling—I'm a hard worker, good listener, and fast learner, which make me a great student.

Showing—I'm highly confident, committed, and motivated, which make me supremely competitive.

Dressage—I'm focused under pressure, optimistic, and patient, which allow me to be my best.

Cross-Country—I'm courageous, and believe in myself and my horse, which make me a dominant competitor.

People Pleasers

These are riders who always try to do well for others—to impress them—or base their identity on outcomes that others admire. This almost always leads to pressure and the *fear of failure*. Instead of being a *people pleaser*, learn to develop a positive self-image so that you can *please yourself*.

Being prepared with a few *pre-determined* positive statements before you encounter stress is a great way to ensure you'll be able to stay *Pressure Proof*. It's best to repeat them out loud and use them whenever you begin to feel doubt, worry, or lose confidence. Another trick to strengthen them is to repeat the statement several times, each time emphasizing a different word in the sentence (start by emphasizing the first word and then repeat the sentence until each word—in order—has received the emphasis). If your sentence has 10 words, repeat it 10 times. You can even use your *self-image statements*—both performance and personality—as the *thought replacement* that follows your *thought stoppers* (for more on this, see p. 118).

Pressure Proof Plan **Self-Image Statement**

Write your *performance statements*:

Schooling _____

Showing _____

Write your *personality statements*:

Schooling _____

Showing _____

Write when you'll use them:

Schooling _____

Showing _____

10 Music Motivation

Music has always helped riders develop a good sense of rhythm, harmony, and tempo—three things that are necessary for balanced riding. Many of us can remember being told to sing songs like, "Row, Row, Row Your Boat," or "Twinkle, Twinkle Little Star," when we were first starting out. Music (or more precisely singing) can also help us remember to breathe when pressure makes many of us forget (seems unusual that breathing would be the one thing we'd decide to give up when things get a bit tough).

Perhaps even more importantly, music can also be used as a *mental motivator* because it has an uncanny way of pulling great emotions out of us. Music can pump

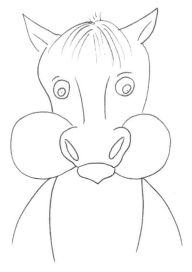

I'm too Busy to Breathe!

us up, calm us down, or make us feel empowered. You might feel bored, lethargic, or otherwise unmotivated, but as soon as you hear your favorite upbeat song you get excited, energized, and inspired. Likewise, you might feel tense, pressured, and rushed but as soon as you hear a favorite calm song, you begin to relax, slow down, and regain your composure.

Musical Memory

Music can help you *remember* important mental or physical skills. For instance, lyrics like, "Be strong, keep pushing on," can remind you to never give up, while lyrics like, "Kick like Adidas, stick like adhesive," can remind you to apply a strong leg aid before a jump then land balanced after it (stick your landing).

Music is considered a *mood modifier* because it can improve the way you feel, and if it can make you feel good, you stand a chance of riding well. When you connect the dots, you'll see that music can, therefore, help you become *Pressure Proof*.

Music has been proven to help athletes compete better, exercise for longer, move faster, and report less perceived exertion and pain. Professional hockey, football, and baseball players even use music as a *purposeful motivator* by picking specific songs to be played during their games—they choose uplifting and energetic songs when they need to get pumped up, and slow ballads when they want to slow the opposing team down. What's more, music isn't just motivational, it's also *inspirational*—that's why so many couples can remember the first time they heard *their song*, even if it was years ago. Music inspires us, triggers memories from our past, and helps us feel good—three things that can certainly lead to great riding.

Create a Playlist

Music has a strange way of getting *stuck in your head* and that's exactly what you should be hoping—getting a favorite song stuck in your thoughts so that its motivating message plays over and over again in your mind. To create your playlist of songs you must first identify your favorite genre of music. For example, is it rock, country, rap, or reggae? Or is it oldies, techno, classical, or pop? Afterward, find a few songs that are meaningful to you. They should make you feel focused, motivated, and energized; make you want to spring out of your chair and ride every time you hear them.

Say what you mean and mean what you say.

Once you've selected your songs, your real work begins because there's much more than music in songs. If you look closely, you might just notice that some of your songs also contain:

Motivation—The rhythm and beat of music can be very motivating. It can pump you up or calm you down, so ask yourself which emotion you need most. You should also take into consideration your riding discipline. Do you need relaxing music to calm you down before dressage; energetic music to pump you up before cross-country; or empowering music to give you a confidence boost just before competing in front of a judge?

Message—If you look closely at lyrics you'll notice that there's often a message contained in them—a form of positive affirmation sentence if you will. For example, the message contained in the lyrics of "The Climb" by Miley Cyrus is:

> *"The struggles I'm facing, the chances I'm taking sometimes might knock me down but I'm not breaking. I may not know it but these are the moments I'm going to remember most, I just got to keep going, got to be strong, just keep pushing on."*

Another example is the message contained in the lyrics for "The Middle" by Jimmy Eats World:

> *"You're in the middle of the ride, everything will be just fine, everything will be all right, just do your best, do everything you can."*

Motto—If you look closely at your song's *message* you might notice that there's a *motivating motto* hidden in the words. Here are a few examples of motivating mottos hidden inside some popular songs: "Keep Calm, Ride On"; "Fight 'Till the End"; "Everything Is Going to Be All Right"; "Nothing's Going to Break My Stride"; "Today Is the Day"; "I've Got the Right Moves";

Our five senses are incomplete without a sixth sense: the sense of laughter!

"Give It Your Best"; "Today Is Your Day"; "Give More Than You Take"; "Just Breathe"; "I Feel Good"; and "Never Say Never."

As great as music is, it does seem to have a pretty short "shelf life," meaning that if you listen to a song too much, it'll soon stop being your favorite. This is called *habituation* and it creates a bit of a challenge. How can you ensure that your songs remain motivational?

The answer is to only listen to them when you really need them. This means that when you hear them on the radio, turn it off. You must purposely withhold your favorite songs until you really need them—like when you're driving to the show grounds and begin feeling your confidence waiver. It's then that you don't just turn your favorite songs on—you turn them up!

When the effectiveness of a song starts to wear off, just remove it from your playlist and replace it with a new one.

Using *music motivation, messages* and *mottos* can help you in many different ways and at many different times: Several hours before a stressful event, motivate yourself by *listening* to your favorite song; five minutes before the event (when you're no longer able to listen to your music), *sing* the music's *message* to yourself; and in the middle of a competition, *say* the music's *motto* as a way of reminding yourself to stay confident and focused (or as a way of recovering after making a mistake).

Another common positive emotion associated with music is *humor*. If you select songs that put you in a good mood and provide you with a little chuckle, they can help keep your thoughts positive. For example, one young rider sings the song, "Best of Both Worlds" because her pony is either too fast *or* too slow; chips in *or* jumps long; rushes fences *or* doesn't jump them at all; comes when she calls *or* runs away! This song reminds her to love her pony regardless of whether she's being good or bad (regardless of which world she comes from).

Another rider sings, "Who Let the Dogs Out" each time she gets nervous when the barn dog appears; another sings, "I'm Sexy and I Know It" each time she begins to doubt herself; and yet another sings the lyrics from "Hall of Fame" ("You can be the greatest, you can be the best, you can be the King Kong beating on your chest!") These riders have figured something out: Music can be a little silly, but a little silly can go a long way to helping you feel positive emotions.

The most unique and special thing about riding is the relationship we share with our horse. Consequently, many riders come up with songs that relate to their horse's name or some other distinguishing feature. The owner of *Sunny* sings, "Walking on Sunshine," the owner of *Fearless* sings, "Fearless," and the owner of a grey sings, "Sitting on the Top of My Grey" (instead of "Sitting on the Dock of the Bay").

Some riding groups sing team songs like, "We Will Rock You" or "We Are the Champions" to get themselves motivated. As with many mental coaching tools you're only limited by your imagination. You can even replace the word "I" with "we" (the song "I Feel Good" becomes "We Feel Good"). Or change the words around a bit: The lyrics "This is going be a good *life*," can become, "This is going be a good *ride*." Here is a list of some other motivating songs from artists of all genres:

- "Wild Horses" by Natasha Bedingfield
- "Today Is Your Day" by Shania Twain
- "Hall of Fame" by The Script
- "Cowgirls Don't Cry" by Brooks and Dunn
- "My Wish" by Rascal Flatts
- "Just Stand Up" by Beyoncé
- "Try" by Pink
- "Who Says" by Selena Gomez
- "Right Now" by Van Halen
- "Hero" by Mariah Carey
- "Win" by Brian McKnight
- "It's My Life" by Bon Jovi
- "Living in the Moment" by Jason Mraz
- "Jump" by Van Halen
- "Nothing's Gonna Break My Stride" by Matthew Wilder
- "The Prayer" by Josh Grogan
- "Born This Way" by Lady Gaga
- "You Gotta Want It" by Jordin Sparks

- "Soar" by Christina Aguilera
- "Cowgirls Don't Cry" by Brooks and Dunn
- "Will to Win" by Team Fredericks (featuring Olympic event rider Clayton Fredericks)

Pressure Proof Plan **Music Motivation**

Write three favorite *pump-up* songs:

(1) _____

(2) _____

(3) _____

Write three favorite *calm-down* songs:

(1) _____

(2) _____

(3) _____

Write two motivating messages:

(1) _____

(2) _____

Write two motivating mottos:

(1) _____

(2) _____

PRESSURE PROOF PROJECT

Rate Your Self-Talk

Answer the following questions to determine if *positive brain babble* can help you improve your riding:

0 = Never   1 = Sometimes   2 = Almost Always

_____ I know what to say to myself to get over a mistake or missed opportunity.

_____ I think positive words to myself when schooling and showing.

_____ I recognize when I'm speaking negatively and can stop it and change it to positive.

_____ I have specific things to say to myself to stay focused and motivated.

_____ I ask myself leading questions and I'm prepared to answer them in a positive way.

_____ My self-talk focuses on my strengths, not my weaknesses.

_____ I'm able to focus my thoughts on the present moment instead of future outcomes.

_____ I'm aware that negative trash talk is contagious so I avoid letting it happen.

_____ I use tools like *motivating cue words, music,* and *mottos* to strengthen my self-talk.

_____ I repeat positive self-image statements to myself.

_____ **Total** (add up your answers).

If your score added up to:

14 to 20

Great—you've learned the value of positive thinking and can use it effectively. There's always room for improvement so continue to think about what you've read in this chapter.

8 to 13

You're on the right track but need more training to make you a more positive rider. Make a list of situations that cause you to think negatively and start improving them by using the tools in this chapter.

0 to 7

Your thinking is predominantly negative: You need a mental-training program to change it to positive. Read this chapter again very carefully, and make a plan to improve your self-talk.

6

Mental Imagery

It's not important what you look at,
but what you see.

A Picture Is Worth a Thousand Words

"A picture is worth a thousand words" is a common saying used to describe the importance of seeing something to really understand it. Trying to explain the massive beauty of the Great Wall of China or the Pyramids of Giza would be difficult—if not impossible—without the help of a few photos. Images created in pictures are able to deliver messages that words simply can't. This is the idea behind *mental imagery:* creating pictures in your mind so that you can clearly understand them (like the artist who creates a mental vision of a painting before he puts brush to canvas).

> **"We don't see things as they are; we see them as we are."**
> — Anais Nin

There's no limit to the different ways you can use *mental imagery*. It can help you:

- Create a mental blueprint of a skill so that you better understand it.

- Identify and correct mistakes.

- Mentally rehearse your courses, tests, or skills.

- Improve your self-confidence (by imagining being confident).

- Improve your motivation (by imagining positive memories).

- Reduce stress (by imagining calm images to slow your heart and respiration rate).

Another interesting way to use imagery is to *mentally* practice skills that may be unsafe or even impossible to *physically* practice. For example, you may not be able to *physically* practice spooking, refusals, or rotational falls, but you can *mentally* rehearse them so that you'll know how to react should they ever occur.

See It to Solve It

When you can *see* a picture of a movement or an imperfection (even if it is only in your mind) you'll have a much better chance of understanding, and therefore, *solving* it. This is why video analysis is such a helpful tool.

 tip   How to Create **Mental Images**

Keep the following in mind:

Relaxation—The more relaxed you are, the faster your mental images become rooted in your subconscious.

Frequency—The more frequently you visualize an image, the stronger it'll become (many short sessions are better than one long session).

Duration—The longer you're able to hold an image the better.

Clarity—The more clear, concise, and visually rich your images, the better.

Present Tense—Your images should remain in the here and now (in the *present-moment mindset*).

Vivid Visualizations

The best images use as many of our five senses as possible: sight, sound, taste, smell, and touch. Each sense is incredibly sensitive, we can see a candle flame from 30 miles on a clear night; hear the tick of a watch from 20 feet; taste a teaspoon of sugar in two gallons of water; smell a drop of perfume in a three-bedroom apartment; and feel the movement of a bee's wing from a half-inch away from our skin.

Emotion—Identify the exact emotions you'll need to succeed and then include them in your images.

Corrective Vision—Visualize solving a problem (for example, if you jump *in front of the motion,* "see yourself" waiting for the fence).

Be Proactive—Create purposeful, positive, and proactive images instead of reactive, random ones.

Pressure Proof **Your Mental Imagery**

1 **Riding Rehearsals**

This common *visualization* technique is used to mentally rehearse an upcoming skill or competition like a dressage test, jumping course, or rein- ing pattern (closing your eyes and seeing the ride in your mind). Using this

Rehearse it in your mind before you ride it on your horse.

technique, you create a sort of mental *highlight film* that reminds you what you must do to ride your best.

When creating your mental highlight film, it helps to start by writing something called an *imagery script*, a detailed list of how you'd like your ride to unfold in your mind. Once you've created your script, you can further increase the effectiveness of your *riding rehearsals*:

1 Push an imaginary *slow-motion* button on your mental *highlight reel* so you can more clearly see how you must perform. This technique can also help you slow the speed of your *riding rehearsal* because, when experiencing stress, it's common for many riders to imagine riding faster than normal.

2 Push an imaginary *freeze-frame* button on your mental *highlight reel* whenever you need to take a closer and longer look at an important aspect of your ride.

3 Remember to make your rehearsals vivid by using your senses: What *sound* does the saddle, tack, and horse make; what do you *see;* how does

---

tip **What to Include in Your Riding Rehearsal**

Surroundings—Where you are, what it looks, sounds, smells, and feels like.

Sensations—How you feel, how your horse moves, and what the sun and wind feel like.

Emotions—Decide how you must feel to ride your best and then act that way while mentally rehearsing your ride.

Brain Babble—Decide what you should be thinking (for example, *cue words* or *mottos*) during your ride and repeat them during your rehearsals.

In Real Time—Mental rehearsals should progress at the same speed as the skill you are imagining. For instance, if your jumping course will take 75 seconds to ride, your *riding rehearsal* should last 75 seconds. But when the discipline lasts too long to imagine (such as in endurance or cross-country), just focus on riding the key elements of the ride in real time.

Start to Finish—Imagine all parts of the show or event (not just the actual competition): Include the warm up, entrance, start, and the way you'll finish.

Repetition—Mentally rehearse your ride as often as possible. The better you train the mind, the better the body will follow.

the wind and sun *feel*; can you *hear* birds singing or a truck coming from behind; and what *sensations* do you *feel* in your legs, back, and heels?

Mind and Body Connection

The idea of *riding rehearsals* isn't a new one. Research using MRI (*Magnetic Resonance Imaging*) technology has shown for years that the chemical, biological, and neurological changes occurring in our body during vivid *riding rehearsals* can be identical to the changes in our body during an actual ride. It's even shown that mental rehearsals can cause our muscles to contract in the same way as they do during a real ride. For example, when the physical demands of your *imagined* ride become more challenging, your muscles will actually contract more.

Through the use of control groups, research has been able to prove that *riding rehearsals* can lead directly to skill development. For example, consider this study: 10 riders practice canter departs; 10 others study and mentally rehearse canter departs; and 10 more sit in a donut shop and do nothing (no cantering, no rehearsing, only eating). After a set period of time

each group is tested and the results show that the riders who simply imagined the canter departs often improved as much as those who actually practiced them. (To no one's surprise, the riders in the third group didn't get any better; they just got fat!) These studies prove that *mental rehearsals* can actually lead to the development of *muscle memory* (successful movements that can be consistently repeated without mental effort) and ultimately improved riding.

Kinds of Riding Rehearsals

When it comes to visualizing your ride, you can use many different *perspectives*. Another way of describing this is imagining your ride as if filming it from different *camera angles*. You have several options:

Internal Perspective—This is called the *associated perspective* and occurs when you imagine seeing your ride from out of your own eyes (as if they are the lens of the camera). You see your horse's ears in front of you and the dressage letter or jump as you approach it.

External Perspective—This is called the *dissociated perspective* and occurs when you imagine seeing your ride from the eyes of others (such as spectators, coaches, judges); from other locations (from a camera suspended over the jump field, for example); or as if watching yourself on TV or seeing

Visualizing your position helps you identify your strengths and weaknesses.

yourself in a photo. This perspective helps you see things more objectively and makes it easier to spot flaws in your mechanics. Visualizing an image in this way can also help you "see" how you've ridden in the past and decide if you need to make any changes in the present or future.

Partner Perspective—This perspective (perhaps the most important of all) takes into consideration all the thoughts and feelings of your horse. Instead of seeing your ride through your own eyes (or the eyes of someone else), imagine it through the eyes of your horse. What must he be thinking when you ask him to jump a 4-foot wooden goose or to trot up the center-line toward a small building with people sitting inside? This perspective is unique to our sport because no other athletes share their playing field with an animal.

Modeling Perspective—In this perspective you visualize someone else with expertise in a skill you'd love to develop. This perspective can also be called *imitation*, *observational learning,* or *mentoring* because you iden-tify someone with great *physical skills* (such as a great jumping position) or *mental strengths* (like focus under pressure) and then imagine making them your own. It's important to remember that you're not comparing yourself to this other rider (or trying to be that person); you're only emulating her skills so that you can develop them.

Matching Perspective—Similar to *modeling*, in this perspective you *match* your riding movement or emotions to those of *something* else (not *some-one* else as in *modeling*). Jumping as if you're a soaring eagle, or observing your course as intensely as an owl, are a couple of examples.

Mental Rotation—This is not really a type of *riding rehearsal* but a com-bination of many. Instead of limiting yourself to a single *perspective* you mentally rotate your camera angles from one perspective to another. For example, a jumper may use the *internal perspective* to visualize the distance to her first fence; the *external perspective* to visualize her equitation over it; the *partner perspective* to visualize what her horse sees on the landing; and then the *modeling perspective* to imagine how her coach would finish strong after pulling a rail on that fence.

Motor Imagery—Perhaps the most effective form of *riding rehearsal*, this technique can be done using any perspective and combines mental rehearsal with a physical movement. Instead of simply *thinking* your riding rehearsal, *move* your body as if you're actually performing it. For example, while visualizing your dressage test, move your hips as if you're sitting the trot up the centerline; open your inside shoulder as you track left around the corner; then apply your inside leg as you transition to a 10-meter circle at "E."

While all mental perspectives can lead to success, the *internal, external,* and *motor imagery* perspectives seem to be the strongest because they've

Biofeedback and Riding Rehearsals

When using a *riding rehearsal* to visualize a mistake, try creating the emotions normally associated with it—like frustration and disappointment. When you've created these feelings, take a deep breath and use a stress management tool like a *motivating motto* or *cue word* to relax and regain a positive frame of mind. The point of using the feedback from your body—or *biofeedback*—is: (1) to teach yourself to recognize the kind of changes that occur in your body when feeling pressure, and (2) to learn what you can do in response to these changes so that you can control them.

been proven to lead to the development of muscle memory (something that until recently was only thought to happen with physical practice). The *partner perspective* is another great choice because it reminds you to take into consideration the thoughts and feelings of your horse (to get the most out of his *body* you must be aware of what's going on in his *mind*).

Perfect and Realistic Riding Rehearsals

Each time you mentally rehearse a ride you have two choices: You can make it a *perfect riding rehearsal* or a *realistic riding rehearsal*.

In a *perfect* riding rehearsal you visualize what you must do to ride your very best: every stride perfectly placed; every transition perfectly executed; and every aid perfectly applied.

In a *realistic* riding rehearsal you visualize yourself riding well, but then imagine encountering frequent challenges and an occasional mistake (like missing a change or making a 10-meter circle a 10-meter "square" instead!). Immediately after the error you imagine yourself confidently coping with it, identifying the cause and solution, then finishing well as a result.

Pressure Proof Plan **Riding Rehearsals**

Write your three favorite riding rehearsal perspectives:

(1) _____

(2) _____

(3) _____

Write out three situations when you'll use these perspectives:

(1) _____

(2) _____

(3) _____

2 Mental Imagery for Skill Development

In addition to mentally rehearsing your ride, *mental imagery* can also help you learn and improve physical skills. Instead of acquiring skills with your body alone, you increase the possibility of developing them by using both mind and body. To understand how this can happen, it helps to know how your brain functions while riding.

Your brain is made up of two separate halves or *hemispheres*. The *left* side of your brain is called the *analyzer* because it analyzes information into lists and makes tasks such as language, sequential planning, logic, computation, and self-instruction possible. This is the portion of your brain that permits you to create positive thinking; set goals; learn new skills by reading; correct flaws by listening; and develop show strategies. When you ride with this part of your brain, your attention is usually focused on learning from past performances or planning for future ones.

Analysis leads to paralysis!

The *right* side of your brain is called the *integrator* because it integrates the mechanical lists formed in your left brain into fluid and automatic movements. It also allows you to think creatively; move effortlessly and purposefully without overanalyzing; orient yourself in space (for example, develop a jumping position); and use mental images. When you ride with this part of your brain, your attention is usually focused on the present moment—not the past or the future.

In order for you to ride your best you need to use both sides of your brain. The most effective way to do this is to learn new skills on the *left* analyzer side and then, as soon as possible, send that information over to the *right* integrator side so that the skill can be integrated into a fluid, and automatic movement (being able to repeat it without having to think about it). When this mechanical list stays on the left side and doesn't get sent over to your right brain, you'll likely end up riding in a mechanical way. Overusing your *analyzer* leads to *overanalyzing,* something that can hold you back from riding in an effortless way.

When you learned the canter depart you had to think of many things, including the job of the inside leg, outside leg, inside rein, outside rein, and seat. While this certainly helped you learn the skill, it probably left you feeling a bit mechanical—that is, until the day you stopped overanalyzing it

Chunking

Chunking is what occurs in your mind when you process a series of mechanical actions into a single automatic routine. You use *chunking* hundreds of times each day—from putting the saddle pad on before the saddle, to putting your socks on before your shoes. In the beginning, you needed to be reminded of these things, but over time they became automatic. For example, when you first learned to canter, you needed to go through a long analytical checklist, but in time your brain *chunked* the many pieces of the list into one single automatic movement. The same thing happened when you first learned to put on a bridle (what piece goes where). It wasn't until after considerable practice that it became automatic. Left to its own devices your brain will *chunk* almost any repeated mechanical list into an automatic behavior.

and just did it. It was then that the canter-depart skill no longer resided in your analytical left brain but in the effortless right brain. And it was then that you truly learned how to transition to the canter.

   Note: It's important to remember that your mind will also *chunk* incorrect mechanical lists into an automatic behavior so you must make sure that you learn skills correctly from the start.

Train Your Right Brain

One of the best ways to train your *right brain* is to get into the habit of thinking in *pictures* while riding. This is where *visualization* and *mental imagery* occur and where you change mechanical and analytical skills to fluid, understandable, automatic, and purposeful movements. Using mental images to learn how to apply the correct amount of rein tension is a good example. You can think of it in mechanical terms as *tighter* or *softer,* or you can visualize Sally Swift's mental image of holding a bird in each hand—not squeezing so hard that you'll hurt them, yet not so softly that they'll fly away. Using images in this way allows you to learn new skills more effectively because they bring your mind and body together as one.

tip   How to Use **Mental Imagery**

- Create good posture by riding with a book on your head.

- Avoid sitting in a "chair seat" because there are thumbtacks sticking out of the cantle.

- Supple your hips at the two-point position by imagining you are dusting off the cantle with your britches.

- Develop a "deep-seat" canter by polishing the cantle with imaginary saddle soap tied to your hips.

- Create balanced and symmetrical shoulders by carrying glasses of water on them.

- Open the inside shoulder around corners by shining a headlight (on your chest) in the direction you're going.

- Point your toes forward in dressage by imagining there are eyeballs on the toes of your boots, which must keep looking forward.

- Keep your knees bent and close your hip angle over jumps by pushing in the bottom drawer of a dresser with your hips.

- Maintain a supple neck and jaw by opening your mouth just enough to let a fly come in.

- Breathe rhythmically by blowing out a *trick* birthday candle (the kind that lights up again).

- Create a long and straight back by imagining someone is pulling upward on your ponytail.

- Give supple rein pressure by squeezing a drop of warm water out of an imaginary sponge.

- Develop a symmetrical seat by sitting on two imaginary hundred-dollar bills—one under each seat bone.

- Develop independent and quiet hands by holding a tray of imaginary drinks while riding.

- Keep your thumbs on top and your fingers supple by holding imaginary ice cream cones.

- Create good leg contact by imagining your legs are the tentacles of an octopus wrapping around your horse.

- Keep your heels down by imagining you're touching your toes to your knees.

- Open your shoulders by imagining a strong wind blowing them open.

Reach Out and Touch Something

Here are a few suggestions to help you create "vivid visualizations":

1 Make Them "Touchable": Create images that you can actually touch. When you do this, the image becomes more real and understandable because it creates a connection between your mind and body. This is called the *mind-body bridge.* For instance, a trainer notices her student's rein contact is too loose so she picks up two small stones from the arena and instructs her to hold the stones—one in each hand—for the remainder of the lesson. The next day the trainer tells his student, "You don't have to hold the stones today, only imagine what they felt like yesterday." Since she'll still have the physical and mental memory of what the stones felt like, this *mental image* will make perfect sense to her today.

2 Make Them Creative: When it comes to creating vivid mental images you're only limited by your imagination so make them as creative as you can. For instance, a trainer might tell a student to open her shoulders by imagining the wind blowing them open, but how can she "touch" this much wind? A windy day or a fan wouldn't be enough but if she were to stick her hand out of the window of a speeding car, she'll feel plenty of wind. The next time she rides she can simply remind herself how it felt to touch "plenty of wind" and how it pushed her hand back.

3 Use All Your Senses: Engaging as many of your senses as possible while imagining your *mental images* makes them feel very lifelike. For instance, a young rider was told to imagine spikes sticking out of her horse's neck to avoid leaning too far forward, but instead of just thinking it, she took a gallon of hair gel and actually spiked her horse's mane! She could now *touch* the pointy parts and *feel* the stickiness of the gel; she could actually *see* the spikes and *smell* them too. All these senses worked together to create a very effective and understandable image.

4 Make Them Funny: Create images that are funny, ridiculous, or just plain weird. When you do this, the images become very memorable. For instance, while imagining you are holding sponges will certainly create good rein tension, holding a hamster in each hand and not squeezing them too hard (or their eyes will pop out!) is a funny example from one young rider. Here are few other examples of funny images:

- **Potty Squat**—A young rider learned her two-point position by imagining she was going to the bathroom in a "porta-potty." The weight's in her heels, knees open, hips back, and *hovering* over the seat (not touching it!), while moving her hands slightly forward to reach for the paper, and never looking down!

- **Beach Ball**—A rider struggling with her sitting trot knew that her tight hips were causing her to bounce (much like the tight outer "skin" of a beach ball causes it to bounce), so she learned to relax her hips by imagining them as two big beach balls with some of the air let out. Since the outer walls of the balls were no longer so tight, there was no bounce left.

• **Wonderbra**—A rider learned to open her shoulders by remembering the well-known slogan of the Wonderbra®. Instead of forcing her shoulders open she simply reminds herself to "lift and separate"!

Pressure Proof Plan **Mental Images for Skill Improvement**

Write three imperfections that affect your riding:

(1) _____

(2) _____

(3) _____

Write the three images that can help you improve them:

(1) _____

(2) _____

(3) _____

3 Memory Motivation

One of the greatest things about riding is that it provides you with years of wonderful memories: times spent with your horse, family, trainers, and riding mates. Thanks to the unique relationship with the horse, your memories often become stronger than the memories of athletes participating in other sports. For instance, you never see a tennis player hugging his racquet, a hockey player taking his stick for a walk, or a skier kissing her skis. Riding is a truly special sport and as a result your memories become just as special. In addition to reminding you of all the amazing things you've experienced in the past, they can also help you create amazing ones in the future.

Positive memories pump you up. Negative memories put you down.

All riders have experienced *memory motivation* at some point in their life. For example, a nervous rider before a show regains her confidence after her coach reminds her how well she did at her last show (even though she was nervous back then, too). This helps her to remember how well she handled the pressure and gives her new confidence in her ability to do it again now. As a result, the memory *motivates* her to remember that she's a capable, strong, and competent competitor. Her coach used *memory motivation* to remind her that a *memory* from her *past* can be used to *motivate* her in the *present*.

Memory Motivation vs. Detachment

Memory motivation is often confused with *detachment* but there is one big difference. In *detachment*, you imagine a *location* that you can basically *escape* to so that you can avoid thinking of the challenge. But in *memory motivation,* you imagine a *memory* from your past that proves you can handle the challenge in the present, right where you are. For instance, you

Make your memories motivational and inspirational.

might imagine *detaching* to a quiet location—like your horse's stall early in the morning—to calm yourself down before a big show. While this may work sometimes, it is—in a way—a form of the defense mechanism *avoidance* (when you can't cope with the pressure where you are, you imagine being somewhere else, even if it's only in your mind).

Whatever emotion you need to create, *memory motivation* can help you achieve it by taking you there mentally. Instead of *detaching* and leav-

How to Build Your Own **Memory Motivation**

Let the following true stories help you. A rider reminds herself:

- To never give up by recalling the memory of her two-year-old daughter yelling, "Go Mommy," as she approached a challenging cross-country fence.

- To trust her horse by remembering a memory when she was afraid her horse would run away with her, but instead, she ended up scoring time faults because they went too slowly!

- How lucky she is by thinking of the time she received a nameplate for the horse she was *about* to receive as a surprise birthday present.

- How hard she's willing to work by recalling the time she traded her pony for a day for an FEI dressage horse that piaffed and passaged without being asked.

- How meaningful her horse is to her by recalling the memory of lying on the ground in a pasture on a sunny day with him happily grazing beside her.

- What fun riding is by remembering playing cops and robbers with a friend and their horses.

- How exciting riding is by thinking of the time she galloped through a field not being able to feel her horse's hooves touching the ground.

- How special the horse-and-rider relationship is by thinking of the way her horse snuggled up to her for warmth on a cold winter day.

- To enjoy herself by remembering the time she walked her horse in the ocean and surfed with him in the waves.

- To forgive by recalling the memory of when her horse spooked and bucked throughout a dressage test after which she laughed and said, "He's a jerk, but he's *my* jerk, and I love him!"

ing a stressful situation emotionally, recall a positive and empowering memory from your past that reminds you you're capable of handling it right here in the present. You allow the positive memory from your *past* to motivate you in the *present*.

Memory motivation works best when you know what makes you nervous. Is it competing in front of a large crowd, being critiqued by a judge, or going last in a class? When you encounter the stressful situation, simply recall a positive memory from your past when you rode well in front of a large crowd; succeeded while being judged; or did great even though you went last in a class. When you're nervous or tense but don't really know why, simply recall a memory from your past when you felt confident. The only thing the memory needs to do is remind you that you already have the mental skills you're looking for.

Your greatest memories might come from the most unusual times!

As you can see, none of these examples focus on winning, standings, or beating another rider. Instead, they simply remind us of our love of riding and horses. While your memories can certainly be about riding well and succeeding (a first victory gallop, for example) they really only need remind you of why you love doing what you do.

Negative Memory Motivation

As positive as *memory motivation* is, it can be used in a negative way if you're not careful (remember to use it for *good*, not *evil*). For

Exception to the Rule

Memory motivation is one of only very few examples when you can think in the *past focused mindset*. In general, you should always keep your focus in the *present* moment and avoid thinking of the past. When the memory you're recalling is a positive and motivating one, however, you can bend this rule a bit.

example, a rider who's not performing up to her potential because she's thinking about a recent fall is using *memory motivation,* but she's using it in a negative way—and it's motivating her in a negative way. Instead of selecting a memory that lifts her up, the memory that's stuck in her mind is pulling her down.

It's not uncommon for negative memories to blind you to the many positive moments and successes that have occurred in your past. Ask any rider who's focused on a negative memory to tell you a positive one and don't be surprised if she can't find one (the negative memory is blinding her to positive ones). The good news is that positive *memory motivation* is just as strong: If you're constantly focusing on positive memories they'll blind you to any negative ones.

When done carefully there are a few positive ways to use negative memories. The first is when you recall something from your past you'd like to avoid in the future. For instance, a rider who used to smoke can recall how hard it was to ride without losing her breath and vow never to go back to her old bad habit again. Secondly, negative memories can sometimes

Mental Focus Test

Look around your room for 10 seconds and make a mental list of everything that's blue: Look at the walls, pictures, furniture, and outside the windows. Close your eyes and think of your list for a few more seconds then quickly name five things that are yellow! If you're like most people you'll probably have a hard time thinking of five yellow things. You focused so hard on blue that you weren't able to see yellow—or anything else for that matter. The same thing happens to you when you focus on a negative memory; you aren't able to see anything else.

be used as learning tools: A jumper who knocks down several fences in her first class (because she rushed them) can use that negative memory to remind herself to ride in a more relaxed and patient manner in her next class. Lastly, some negative memories can be used to help you avoid harm. For example, a rider who had a bad fall when her horse spooked at a tractor can keep herself safe in the future by recalling the negative memory and dismounting whenever a tractor passes by.

Success Soundtrack

Imagining your positive *memory motivation* at the same time as listening to (or thinking of) your *music motivation* results in something called a *success soundtrack*: motivating images set to motivating music much like a movie trailer.

In the end, however, the benefits of *positive-memory motivation* far outweigh those of *negative-memory motivation* so they should make up the vast majority of your *memory motivation* program.

Pressure Proof Plan **Memory Motivation**

Write down one *pump-up* motivating memory:

_____

_____

_____

Write down one *calm-down* motivating memory:

_____

_____

_____

PRESSURE PROOF PROJECT

Rate Your Mental Imagery Skills

Answer the following questions to determine if *mental imagery* can help you improve your riding:

0 = Never   1 = Sometimes   2 = Almost Always

_____ I use mental images to learn new skills or improve old ones.

_____ When using mental images I use as many of my senses as possible.

_____ I make my images memorable by making them humorous and "touchable."

_____ I use mental images to rehearse my jumping course, dressage test, or reining pattern.

_____ I use different perspectives when imaging my rides (*internal, external, partner, modeling, matching, mental rotation, motor imagery, perfect,* and *realistic*).

_____ My *riding rehearsals* progress at the same pace as my actual ride.

_____ I imagine *positive memories* as a way of motivating myself.

_____ I use mental imagery in a lesson as well as in competition.

_____ When I'm nervous or tense I visualize calm images to relax myself.

_____ When I'm unmotivated I visualize exciting images to pump myself up.

_____ **Total** (add up your answers).

If your score added up to:

14 to 20

Great—you've learned the value of mental imagery and can use it effectively. There's always room for improvement so continue to think about what you read in this chapter.

8 to 13

You're on the right track but need more training to make you a more visual rider. Make a list of ways to use mental imagery and begin today.

0 to 7

You are struggling and need a mental-training program to improve your mental imagery. Read this chapter again very carefully, and make a plan that will include plenty of vivid visualization.

7

Goal Setting

Dreams are where you want to end up.
Goals are how you get there.

Begin with the End in Mind

Riding is a very goal-oriented activity. Regardless of whether you're learning to jump, training a young horse, moving up through the levels, or developing a conditioning program, setting goals should be an important part of everything you do. In addition to helping you become *Pressure Proof*, goals help you use your training time more efficiently; focus on what's most important; find strategies that lead to success; provide feedback on your progress; and give you reasons to keep going.

Goals also provide you with a clear vision of what you'd love to accomplish (if you don't know where you're going you're going to have a hard time getting there). In some ways, goal setting can be considered a *map to success*—your long-term goal is the destination and your

short-term goals are the step-by-step directions telling you how to get there.

Kinds of Goals

1 Short-Term Goals—Often referred to as *process goals*, *short-term* goals create a series of specific steps and actions (a *process*) that need to happen in order for you to ride and compete your best. Instead of focusing on the *outcome* of an event (like a ribbon, final placing, or a podium finish) these goals help you focus on the many *processes* that create the possibility of riding so well that you *earn* the desired successful outcome. That means, instead of focusing on the outcome, you focus on what you can do to create it. For example, if you know you'll need precise transitions and good lateral work in a future dressage test, you set them as your *short-term* goals and develop them, knowing that when you do, you'll have a greater chance of creating the success you desire.

Short-term goals create long-term improvements.

There are three different kinds of *short-term* goals:

Behavioral—like arriving on time for every lesson and respecting your coaches.

Emotional—like thinking positively, riding with confidence, and maintaining focus.

Technical—like balancing your corners, landing "in your heels," and seeing your distances.

2 Long-Term Goals—Often called *product goals,* these goals are result-oriented goals that are clearly measurable and remind you of the meaningful things you'd love to accomplish in the near (or distant) future. Goals such as moving up to Training Level in eventing next fall; scoring an average of 65 percent or higher in dressage this summer; or competing in at least five recognized horse shows this year are all good examples of *product* goals.

Long-term goals are best when set pre- and post-season; when they can be accomplished within six to 12 months; and when they are limited to three each competition season. You can also set up to three additional *long-term* goals for any off season—goals such as losing 10 pounds before April; participating in a strength-and-conditioning program this winter; or teaching your horse his changes before next season.

Many riding associations are set up to use *long-term* goals as a way of keeping their riders motivated and on track during long seasons. The U.S. Pony Club, for example, awards their riders with a letter rating from D to A as they improve (much like karate awards athletes different colored belts). It's the constant desire to move up to the next rating that keeps these great young riders motivated and on track.

> **"Goals are dreams with a deadline."**
> — Napoleon Hill

3 Outcome Goals—Unlike positive *short-* and *long-term* goals, *outcome* goals are negative and thus should be avoided because they force you to focus on winning, beating a competitor, standings, rankings, or the color of the ribbon. While these goals are tempting (because positive outcomes are closely associated with winning) they don't tell you anything about how to achieve the success.

Perhaps the greatest problem with *outcome* goals is that they force you to compare your performance and potential to others, meaning that you aren't just thinking about how well you'll do, but how well everyone else will do, as well. As a result, *outcome* goals are clearly out of your control: You have no control over the talent of other riders, the opinions of the

It's not the color of the ribbon, but the ~~quality~~ of the ride. Having said that, I'd like a blue one, please.

judge, or the quality of the other horses, so focusing on them is an unfortunate waste of time and effort.

While there certainly are plenty of things out of your control, there are just as many things within your control: Your *behaviors, emotions,* and *techniques* are just a few of them. When you focus on these *processes* that create success, you remain in the "positive" *present-state* mindset instead of the "negative" *future-state* mindset (hoping you'll achieve a particular outcome in the future). When it comes to goal setting, remember that a successful outcome shouldn't be considered a goal; instead think of it as the *reward* for achieving your short- and long-term goals. The more you focus on the outcome, the further you'll be from achieving it.

Getting a ribbon is the reward for setting and achieving goals.

It's very important to remember that your mind can really only consciously focus on one thing at a time. When it's focused on the *outcome* it can't be focused on the many steps and actions (the processes) that can create it.

Pressure Proof **Your Goal Setting**

1 **Setting Goals**

If you're not sure where you're going, you'll probably end up somewhere else.

Anyone who's ever made a New Year's resolution knows that setting a goal is easy but achieving it can be very hard. Perhaps this is why only about 13 percent of people who resolve to lose weight actually do so, and why about 50 percent of those who begin an exercise program stop it within six months. Setting goals is important but achieving them is just as important. Below is a list of tips you can use to make sure you don't just set goals, but achieve them as well.

 The Best Kinds of **Goals**

Ideally, goals should be:

Motivating—Set a combination of *short-* and *long-term* goals to help you stay focused and motivated, and that will give structure to your training and showing programs. These goals will help you focus on your own behaviors, emotions, and techniques—not on the behaviors, emotions, and techniques of others. They can also teach you to love the journey just as much as the destination—the battle just as much as the victory.

Worthwhile—Goal setting requires hard work and dedication so your goals should make the sacrifices worthwhile. Setting average goals creates average results—setting exciting and meaningful goals create exciting and meaningful results.

> "The greatest risk for most of us lies not in setting our aim too high and falling short; but in setting our aim too low and achieving our mark."
>
> — Michelangelo

Realistic—Always set goals that are challenging but achievable; they should encourage you to grow, to push and test yourself, and get you out of your comfort zone. The best goals are those that you're 60 to 80 percent certain you can achieve. When they're too ambitious, you risk becoming frustrated or disappointed, and when they're too easy, you risk losing motivation.

Self-Determined—Your goals should be *all about you*; they should be meaningful to you not meaningful to someone else. Always set goals that you want (when someone else tells you what goals to set, the chance of achieving them drops), and avoid setting goals just to make others happy (coach, trainer, or family). For a goal to be motivational, it must make *you* happy.

Action-Oriented—In a strange way goals are like verbs because they're "action" words. They're not static, inactive or unchanging, but instead are a dynamic, active, and ever-changing series of steps and actions that can help you achieve a desired outcome. Being prepared to modify and adapt your *short-term* goals proves that you're willing to do anything to achieve your *long-term* ones.

One at a Time—Setting goals works best when you limit yourself to no more than three *long-term* goals per season. If you set too many at once it can bog you down and make it difficult to focus your full attention on any of them. The more you set, the less likely you'll achieve them—*quality* is definitely better than *quantity*.

Positive—It's easy to set goals in a *negative* way because it's often easier to know what you *don't* want (to have happen) than to know what you *do* want to happen (not forgetting your course or not finishing last in a class). Goals should be voiced in a positive way by avoiding the word *not* and by focusing on the many positive things you *do* want to happen.

Set for Schooling and Showing—Many riders set goals for competition but forget to set goals for training. Since training is where the vast majority of all learning takes place, it's important to use goals to create a positive structure and focus for all your lessons.

Specific—Avoid setting ambiguous goals: The more specific and concise they are the greater chance they'll have of providing direction and motivation. If you think your goals can be more specific, they probably can be.

How specific should goals be?

Can you be more specific?

Measurable—Goals should allow you to determine whether or not you've achieved them. Non-measureable goals like "trying my best" leave too much up to interpretation (*best* may mean different things to different riders). Measurable goals like "to jump clear" are more productive because they let you know when you've achieved them—or not.

The best way to predict success in the future is to start creating it today.

"Time Bound"—Creating a target date for your goals helps you to avoid procrastination or become complacent. You can avoid this by setting a date and sticking with it. If your goal isn't achieved by the date, allow yourself an extension. Remember that there are very few unrealistic goals, only unrealistic time frames to accomplish them!

Believable—When the gap between your ability and your goal is too big, your mind won't be able to accept the discrepancy (say, a novice rider who hopes to ride in the Olympics in four years). This doesn't mean it's impossible, only that you might need to make a few adjustments to the goal or its target date.

> "Obstacles are the things you see when you take your eyes off your goals."
>
> — Henry Ford

Perpetual—A goal that requires a lifetime commitment is fine but goals tend to be more achievable when you work on them one day at a time. A rider telling herself to quit smoking for the rest of her life may struggle with the enormity of her decision, but if she sets many consecutive goals of giving up smoking—for one day only—her chance of sticking to it will increase.

Ethical—Always set goals that are consistent with your values and morals. If your goals go against them (such as sacrificing your horse's safety for a ribbon) you'll be disappointed in yourself because it wasn't worth it. Linking your goals to your values helps you become the best rider possible and this is what makes goal setting so meaningful.

"This would be a whole lot easier if I had thumbs!"

2 Keep a Record

Writing your goals on paper will make them "feel" more real and important; it helps provide you with a physical tool for focusing your attention on them. Some studies even show that you're up to 10 times more likely to achieve goals that are written down than those that aren't—out of sight, out of mind. Written goals can also help you measure your progress (like a score card), encourage you to become more accountable for your actions, and provide you with a kind of visual motivation and structure that can lead to greater goal achievement.

For many people, when you want to remember something you had better write it down. How many times have you arrived at the grocery store without your shopping list only to realize that you have no idea what you were supposed to buy? Writing a shopping list makes certain you'll come home with what you wanted instead of wondering, "What am I doing with light bulbs when I went out to buy milk?"

Writing your goals down on paper also stimulates a portion of your brain called the *reticular activating system,* the same area responsible for awareness. This means that writing goals not only makes them more memorable, it also makes you more conscious and *aware* of them. It stimulates the portions of your brain responsible for thinking, seeing, and writing. Read the words of your goals out loud and the areas of the brain that control speech and hearing will also be engaged. Obviously, the more areas of the brain you stimulate the more effective your goals will become. As if this wasn't enough, seeing written goals that you've already achieved can improve your confidence because you're able to see all your current and past accomplishments.

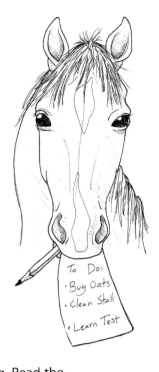

Goal setting: The "write" to remember.

Prepare to Modify Your Goals

Some riders write their goals with a large felt marker (so the words "jump" off the page) while others write them in pencil so they can easily erase and change them, if needed. Regardless of the writing instrument, one thing is certain: You must be prepared to modify your goals from time to time.

Remember that changing them is not a sign of failure but a way of taking into consideration new information that you didn't have when you originally set them. When you set your goals in stone and aren't prepared to change them, you eliminate the chance of learning from the new information, which lessens your chance of achieving your goals.

For example, if a rider's goal is to jump clear, she'll likely feel disappointed when she pulls the first rail and isn't prepared to modify the goal. On the other hand, when she imagines her goal written in pencil (erasable) and is prepared to modify it, she can quickly change the goal from having a clear round to having a "clear-ish" round. This could again be changed to having a strong finish after a slow start, which could again be changed to something else like just getting out of the arena alive!

Making a Goal-Setting Journal

Keeping a goal-setting journal can provide you with a structured way to catalog your progress toward your goals as well as the thoughts and feelings you have along the way. Ideally your journal should include the following:

- The date.
- Type of activity (schooling or showing).
- The goals for the activity.
- Thoughts, feelings, and motivation before, during, and after the activity.
- Mental strategies employed during the activity and their effectiveness.
- Performance rating (how well you think you did in your goal quest).
- Ideas/comments/observations (like what you learned and what you should do next time).

3 Goal-Setting Ladder

Once you've written your goals on paper, consider sharing them with your trainer, riding peer, or family. This is called *publishing your goal* and is a good idea because it can increase your sense of accountability as well as provide you with the feeling that if you forget them someone will remind you. You can also consider creating a list of resources (books, CDs, clinics, seminars) that can help you reach your goals; a list of possible obstacles that might stand in your way (so they won't be such a surprise if they happen); and a list of strategies (and priorities) that can help you achieve your goals. One such strategy is called a *goal-setting ladder*.

Build the Ladder

Step One—Take a piece of paper and draw a ladder on the left half of the page. At the top of the ladder write one *long-term* goal that you'd love to accomplish in the near or distant future. You should make it moderately difficult but attainable (remember that you should be 60 to 80 percent sure you can reach it).

Step Two—With the exception of the lowest step (starting with the second lowest rung), write one *short-term* goal on each rung of the ladder. You'll notice that each one will take you one step closer to the top of the ladder and your *long-term* goal. These short-term goals can consist of *behavioral, emotional,* and *technical* goals and should be listed in chronological order starting with the most recent on the bottom.

Step Three—On the lowest rung of the ladder, write an *immediate goal*. This is a goal that will act as the spark to ignite your desire to start climbing up toward your *long-term* goal. For example, if your *long-term* goal is to attend a clinic with an Olympic rider, your immediate goal would be to go to his website to see when he'll be teaching in your area. This is a very important step because it's what really gets the ball rolling.

Step Four—Once your *immediate, short-* and *long-term* goals are on your ladder, attach a target date to each of them. The

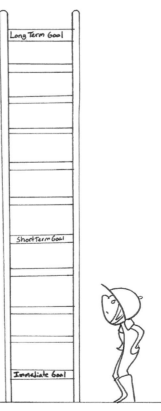

long-term goal should be achieved within the next six to twelve months; each *short-term* goal within a two-to-four week period; and your *immediate* goal by the end of the day.

Step Five—Beside your ladder on the right side of you page, make a list of your *short-term* goals then write one *specific* and *measurable* strategy that will help you attain each one.

A matter of <u>will</u> is as important as a matter of <u>skill</u>.

Step Six—Once your ladder and list of strategies are completed, take it and place it somewhere you'll see it throughout the day—every day. It can be taped to your fridge, bathroom mirror, on the wall of the tack room, or on the lid of your tack trunk. It's not important where, it's just important that it's in a place where you'll see it often.

The purpose of the *goal-setting ladder* is to remind you that there's only one way to the top—*one step at a time* (one *short-term* goal at a time). If you get impatient and try jumping from the ground to your *long-term* goal (the top rung), chances are pretty good you'll end up feeling disappointed, defeated, dejected, and depressed (the "D" words). For example, if you're currently a walk-trot rider with a *long-term* goal of jumping cross-country, it might not be a good idea to start cantering over banks and chicken coops today!

4 Why Riders Avoid Setting Goals

The benefits of goals are clear, so why do so many riders hesitate to set them? Perhaps knowing what the common reasons are will help to convince you that the benefits far outweigh the challenges:

1 Fear of Failure—The first reason many riders hesitate to set goals is because they want to avoid the disappointment of not being able to achieve them. This is considered a *fear of failure* because they find it more acceptable to *not try*, than to risk failing.

> "What you get by achieving your goals is not as important as what you become by achieving them."
> — Henry David Thoreau

2 Fear of Success—The opposite of a fear of failure is a *fear of success*. This occurwhen a rider achieves an important goal then feels that she'll need to keep achieving goals in the future or else be labeled as a slacker.

3 Impressions—Some riders hesitate to set goals because they believe their peers will think badly about their "weird" way of training, or that they are trying to go beyond being average. These are typically the same riders who feel that they need to apologize for their success.

4 Lack of Willpower—Sometimes riders are just not willing to put in the time or effort to achieve a goal. *Willpower* is defined as having the self-control to resist immediate or instant gratification in order to achieve a long-term goal. Some riders incorrectly believe that setting goals requires too much time and doubt that the effort they put in today will benefit them tomorrow. When done correctly, goal setting can actually be a timesaver because it gives your training sessions greater structure and purpose, and makes them more efficient by focusing more of your time on the skills that'll benefit you the most.

Any goal worth setting is a goal worth working and waiting for.

5 Wrong Tool for the Right Job—Many riders struggle with goals because they set the wrong kind. Instead of setting positive, *short-* and *long-term process* goals, they set *outcome* goals and quickly end up feeling frustrated as they fall short of achieving them.

6 Lack of Interest—Sometimes riders just don't find goal setting very exciting. Learning to set effective *short-* and *long-term* goals and feeling the joy and reward of achieving them should be reward enough and make up for any lack of excitement.

tip How to Motivate Yourself to Achieve Your Goals

The "How Come?" Technique—Think about your most meaningful *long-term* goal then ask yourself, "How come I haven't done it yet?" Then arrive at two or three answers to the question (the answer will provide you with information on how to achieve it). For example, if your goal is to learn how to jump, and you ask, "Why haven't I done it yet?" the answer might be something like, "I don't have an instructor, or the right tack or horse for jumping."

If you aim at nothing at all, you'll hit the target every time.

Armed with this information you can now set out to achieve it by locating a local jumping barn with instructors and school horses. In this way, the answers to your questions point you in the right direction and help you form a strategy to achieve the goal.

Goal Reminder—Surround yourself with visual reminders that help you remember and remain focused on your goals. For example, when your goal is to lose weight, you can place an old picture of yourself on the fridge when you were 20 pounds lighter as a visual reminder of your weight-loss goal. You're only limited by your own creativity—the more meaningful the reminder and the more you see it, the more likely you'll be motivated to achieve it.

Goal Poster—This is like the *goal reminder* only larger and more visually stimulating. If your goal is to move up to Fourth Level dressage, make a poster containing many different kinds of visual motivators such as photos of you schooling a Fourth Level movement; a magazine photo of your favorite rider going Fourth Level; a quote from a riding mentor about moving up in dressage; the name of a show that you aspire to compete at Fourth Level; and a *motivating motto* printed in big bold ink. In the middle of the poster you can put your *goal-setting ladder* describing the *immediate* and *short-term* steps you plan on using to reach Fourth Level.

Don't go through life.
Grow through life.

Another interesting way to make a *goal poster* is to put your visual motivators on the border of a mirror. The next time you see yourself in the mirror, you'll be reminded how important the goal is to you.

Reward—Motivate yourself to achieve a meaningful goal by tempting yourself with a reward when you succeed. The reward can be:

- *Material,* like a new halter, boots, or saddle. It works best when you have needed something but have delayed buying it until you achieve your goal.

- *Experiential,* like a telling yourself that you'll take your horse on a wonderful trail ride in the countryside or go on a riding vacation as soon as you achieve your goal.

- *Intrinsic,* like the feeling of accomplishment you know you'll feel when you achieve it (or the pride you'll take when you're able to cross it off your list).

Regardless of the reward, it's important that the reward be meaningful and delivered as soon after the completion of your goal as possible.

Reverse Reward—Instead of rewarding yourself with something positive, you motivate yourself by setting a *negative reward* (to be delivered if you

> **"You don't have to be great to start, but you have to start to be great."**
> — Joe Sabah

give up before it's accomplished). For example, if you're a vegetarian you could tell yourself that if you give up before achieving your goal you will have to make a $20 donation to the American Beef Association! It's amazing how effective this form of *reverse motivation* can be.

Journal—As mentioned earlier in the chapter, get in the habit of writing your goals in a journal so you can follow your progress. This is a great way of keeping on track and remaining motivated. Each time you cross off a *short-term* goal, move down the page to the next one, and each time you achieve a *long-term* goal, write down a new one. Putting your *goal-setting ladder* on the front cover or on the

"C" Your Goals

In the *brain babble* chapter (p. 103), you learned how "C" emotions can create positive thoughts and how "D" emotions can create negative ones. *Goal-setting* works much the same way, setting *productive* and *achievable* goals to help you feel confident, competent, consistent, creative, capable, committed, and competitive; while setting goals that are too *difficult* or *out of your control* leave you feeling disappointed, discouraged, depressed, and defeated.

Setting improper goals can also lead to *negative* brain babble: For example, if a rider's only goal is to win, she may speak negatively to herself each time she finishes second. Negative brain babble like, "I'm no good," is certainly poor self-talk, but it's possible that it could also be a sign of poor *goal-setting*—when a rider avoids setting unreasonable goals she'll also likely avoid the negative self-talk that follows.

first page is a good way of reminding yourself how everything will come together in the end.

Win vs. Winning Attitudes

Believe it or not, working toward goals has actually been proven to deliver more motivation and happiness than achieving them. It appears that we're easily inspired by goals because they can provide us with a clear message that we're improving and on the right track. Instead of a *win* attitude (focusing on winning, losing, or the color of the ribbon), goals help you to develop a *winning* attitude (focusing on the many processes that can lead to success).

Rarely do we hear great riders say things like, "If I don't win I'm going to quit because the only important thing is winning." Instead, they say things like, "I've ridden well here in the past and look forward to using that experience to ride well here again today, and also look forward to learning from other great competitors." Riders with a *winning* attitude prove that greatness comes from focusing on the *short-* and *long-term* goals that create success rather than on the *outcome* itself.

5 Legacy Goals

The goals you achieve today create your legacy tomorrow.

Perhaps the most important goal of all, a *legacy goal*, is the culmination of all the meaningful things you wish to accomplish in your riding life and how you plan on achieving them. What achievements would you love to hang on your tack-room wall and what reputation would you love to develop by the end of your riding career? If all your friends and family got together to celebrate your life as an equestrian, what would they say? Would they say that you dedicated yourself to the betterment of horses everywhere; that you worked tirelessly to mentor young riders; or

> "Twenty years from now, you'll be more disappointed by the things you didn't do, than by the ones you did do."
> — Mark Twain

that you never gave up when things got tough? If so, use these kinds of inspirational acts to create your *legacy goal*. Below are a couple examples:

My legacy goals are to become a dedicated equestrian who always believed in my ability to overcome emotional obstacles; devoted myself to helping others do the same; inspired young riders to find their love of riding; and worked tirelessly to ensure my horses received the level of care and devotion they deserved.

My legacy goals are to become a talented equestrian, dedicated horsewoman, knowledgeable trainer, and lifelong mentor and to use these skills and commitment to keep my horses and students safe, healthy, and successful throughout a lifetime of schooling and showing experiences.

Earlier in this chapter I suggested that you write your *short-* and *long-term* goals in pencil so that you can erase and change them if needed. In a sport as unpredictable as riding, you must be prepared to *change* your goals when situations *change*. When it comes to your *legacy goal*, however, you can write it in pen because *no one* and *nothing*—not your opponents, the weather, or number of ribbons—can interfere with your ability to achieve it. It's your own *legacy*: It defines who you are, what you believe in, and what you stand for. You might struggle achieving your *short-* and *long-term* goals from time to time, but every one of your accomplishments and failures brings you one step closer to realizing your *legacy goal*.

So write your *legacy goal* in big bold ink so that it pops off the paper. Or, go to your computer

Exception to the Rule

A *legacy goal* is one of the very few instances when you should think of the *future*. In general, you should always keep your focus in the *present* moment and avoid thinking of the future. When you live your life one day at a time and in such a way that you create a meaningful legacy, you can bend this rule a bit.

and type it in your favorite font, add a meaningful photo or quote, print it in full color, frame it, and hang it somewhere you'll see every day. Repeat it over and over until you commit it to memory and remind yourself that true riding success will be measured at the end of your riding career—not at its peak—and certainly not on one afternoon.

Pressure Proof Plan **Goal-Setting Ladder**

Write a *long-term* goal and its potential completion date:

(1) _____

Write five *short-term* goals that will help achieve it:

(1) _____

(2) _____

(3) _____

(4) _____

(5) _____

Write down one *immediate* goal that will get you started:

(1) _____

Pressure Proof Plan **Legacy Goal**

Write one reason why riding is so meaningful to you:

(1) _____

_____

Write the five most important things to you in riding:

(1) _____

(2) _____

(3) _____

(4) _____

(5) _____

Combine them to make one *legacy goal:*

(1) _____

_____

PRESSURE PROOF PROJECT

Rate Your Goal-Setting Skills

Answer the following questions to determine if goal setting can help you improve your riding:

0 = Never   1 = Sometimes   2 = Almost Always

_____ I use long-term *product* goals to stay focused.

_____ I set short-term *process* goals to achieve my long-term goals.

_____ My goals are challenging but achievable.

_____ I use a goal-setting journal to document my goals.

_____ I reward myself each time I achieve a goal.

_____ My goals are specific, measurable, and timely.

_____ I use tools like *goal reminders*.

_____ I have the willpower to put off instant gratification instead of long-term success.

_____ I set goals for schooling and showing.

_____ I set legacy goals.

_____ **Total** (add up your answers).

If your score added up to:

14 to 20
Great—you've learned the value of goal setting and can use it effectively. There's always room for improvement so continue to think about what you read in this chapter.

8 to 13
You're on the right track but need more training to make your goal setting more effective. Make a list of goals you'd love to achieve and start working toward them using the tools in this chapter.

0 to 7
You're not using goal setting to the best of your ability, so create a mental-training program that will help you improve. Read this chapter again very carefully and start your goal-setting plan today.

8

Stress Management

"Adversity causes some riders to break, others to break records." —William Arthur Ward

Stress and Riding

All riders feel stress from time to time; the difference between good riders and great riders is that the great ones have simply learned how to *manage* it. You can't eliminate stress; it's an inherent part of riding and showing so you must instead learn how to control it rather than trying to avoid it. This is what being *Pressure Proof* is all about.

There's no such thing as stress *elimination* techniques; only stress *management* techniques (learning to *manage* stress instead of fearing it). For instance, if a dressage judge makes you nervous, you could ask her to turn around and not look (good luck trying to *avoid* or *eliminate* the stress this way!), or you can learn to *manage* and *control* it by using the many of tools and techniques described in this book.

Stress isn't just an inherent part of riding, it's actually an important part of it. As mentioned earlier, some stress is usually required for you

Arousal

Apathy

Anxiety

to perform your best. You must feel aroused, excited, engaged, and exhilarated, and the correct amount of *stress* provides this for you. This is often referred to as the "butterflies"—the feeling that you're looking forward to the challenge and that you're confident you can rise to the occasion.

When you have too much stress, however, the butterflies turn into "horseflies" churning inside your stomach making you feel nervous and tense. When you don't have enough stress, the butterflies turn into tiny "fruit flies" leaving you feeling unmotivated and lethargic. The words *anxiety, apathy,* and *arousal* sum up these situations well: When you feel too much stress you become *anxious* (horseflies); not enough, you become *apathetic* (fruit flies); just the right amount and you feel *aroused* (butterflies).

Stress doesn't close doors without first opening a few windows.

Distress vs. Eustress

In addition to managing the *amount* of stress, you must also manage the *type* of stress. There are two different kinds of stress:

Distress is the negative form that makes you panic and rush, feel show jitters, and consider quitting. This is also the kind of stress associated with illnesses like cancer, asthma, ulcers, cardiovascular disease, depression, and hypertension (some studies show that up to 90 percent of all illnesses can be linked, at least partially, to *distress*). These are the "horseflies" of stress and it's important to know that your mind and body do not differentiate between *real stress* (an accident involving your horse trailer for instance), and *imagined* or *anticipated stress* such as competition jitters. They will react to both forms of stress in the same negative way.

The second kind of stress is the lesser-known *eustress*. This is the positive kind that makes you want to get up instead of give up. This is the "butterflies," and it is the kind of stress that's required for you to ride your best. Each of the following techniques (all described in previous chapters) can be used to create this kind of positive stress:

> "When you reach the end of your rope, tie a knot and hang on."
> — Thomas Jefferson

- Positive Self-Talk (p. 107)
- Cue Words (p. 115)
- Thought Stopping (p. 118)
- Thought Replacement (p. 118)
- Question Suggestion (p. 121)
- Relaxation Techniques (p. 209)
- Showing Mindset (p. 56)
- Five Rs of Recovering after Mistakes (p. 86)
- Simulation Training (p. 57)

- "C" ing Is Believing (p. 124)
- Motivating Mottos (p. 128)
- Positive Self-Image Statements (p. 130)
- Motivating Music (p. 133)
- Riding Rehearsals (p. 145)
- Mental Imagery (p. 143)
- Memory Motivation (p. 160)
- Goal Setting (p. 173)

Causes of Stress

A very common cause of stress is the perception that you are out of control. The solution, therefore, is to learn how to *gain* control, *maintain* control and if you ever lose it, *regain* control. This is what *stress management* is all about: Developing the perception of control regardless of the situation or challenge.

Control

Is control important? If you've ever lost the remote control to your TV you've probably realized how important it was. Without it you might panic, blame everyone for losing it, and worry that you'll miss your program—all in the same amount of time that it would have taken to simply get up off the chair and push the button on the TV itself!

In addition to feeling out of control, there are several other factors that can create stress:

- **Change**—Unexpected, or even expected change can play a role in the creation of stress. In fact, the majority of life's greatest stresses, including marriage, moving, divorce, loss of a loved one, or changing jobs, are caused by having to make a change that can temporarily leave you feeling a bit out of control.

- **Perfectionism**—Striving for perfection or focusing on standings and outcomes.

- **Past-Focused Mindset**—Focusing on previous mistakes or missed opportunities.

- **Future-Focused Mindset**—Focusing on future outcomes, standings, and winning.

- **Distractions**—Focusing on distractions that are out of your control.

Law of Impermanence

Nothing stays the same. The world around us is constantly changing and our sport and our horses are no exception. As long as we're prepared for—and accept—change, we will be fine. If we try to stop the wheels of change, however, we get ourselves into trouble. Learn to embrace and seek out change, and make sure that every one is a positive one.

- **Expectations**—Worrying about what others think, not letting them down or not living up to their expectations.

- **Fear of Failure**—Worrying about no being "up to the challenge" or riding below your potential.

- **Loss of Confidence**—Starting poorly and not being able to catch up, starting strongly but letting it slip away, and choking can weaken your confidence and cause stress.

As you can see from this list, many causes of stress have already been mentioned in this book. Not surprisingly, they were discussed in the chapter on negative mental traits (see p. 71). Luckily, there are just as many ways to control stress, as there are causes for it. For the remainder of this chapter I'll discuss the many ways to *gain*, *maintain,* and (if needed) *regain* control of stress. They include *stress-stoppers, toughness training, desensitization, targeting, relaxation techniques, deep breathing,* and *pre-competition routines.*

Equine Stress

Horses also suffer from stress. The main causes of equine stress are being separated from pasture mates; loading; hauling; competing; disruption of routine and diet; changes in turnout schedule; new surroundings; and an inability to graze. It's obvious that *change* and *loss of control* also contribute to equine stress.

Pressure Proof **Your Stress Management**

1 Stress-Stopper

You may not always be able to *stop* stress, but you can certainly learn to control it so that you can *stop the effects* it has on you. This is where *stress-stoppers* come in: positive and controllable habits, behaviors, rituals, or even superstitions that help you create the perception of control.

"I'm not nervous! What makes you think I'm nervous!?"

For example, some riders must wear two different colored socks when they compete. As long as they're able to do so, everything feels fine but if they're forced to wear two same-colored socks they get a little worried. Another rider carries a map of her jump course in her pocket while riding because she believes it helps her remember it. A third rider always arrives at the last second because she knows she'll be more motivated then. The socks, the map, and the last-minute arrival have become the *stress-stoppers* that make these riders feel in control of something—even if it's just their socks, the course, or their preparation.

All elite athletes are trained to use *stress-stoppers*: Basketball players bounce the ball in a specific and repetitive way before attempting a game-winning free throw; tennis players tap the ball on the ground with their racquet in the same repetitive way before each serve; and baseball players hit the home plate and shoes with their bat in

Psychosomatic Symptoms of Stress

When stress or pressure gets to be too much for your brain to handle it can overflow into your body. You can probably remember the unusual experience of waiting to write an important exam and noticing that your palms were sweaty. (When your mind feels too much stress, water starts spurting out of your hands!)

This kind of unusual physical reaction to mental stress is called a *psychosomatic symptom of stress*. Unlike normal *cognitive anxiety* (the kind of stress you feel in your mind) *somatic anxiety* is the kind that you feel in your body. Dry mouth, rapid heart rate, sweating, an upset stomach, vomiting, quickened speech, and jittery movement are a few other examples of physical symptoms that indicate mental stress.

the same specific, repetitive way before each pitch. These *stress-stoppers* help athletes create the perception of control by actually giving them something to control.

When it comes to creating *stress-stoppers* you can be as creative as you want. One young rider writes the number 326 on her hand to remind herself how happy she was when her parents bought her horse on March 26; another rubs the St. Christopher medallion on her necklace while repeating a motivating verse from the Bible; another makes herself smile by stroking her horse's "moustache" each time she gets nervous; and yet another pushes a small white spot on her horse's nose as if it were a STOP (the stress) button each time she gets nervous.

When these riders feel pressure or start thinking negatively they look at their 326, rub their medallion, stroke the horse's moustache, or push the button. As soon as they do, they take a deep breath and repeat a *motivating motto* so they can regain control of themselves, knowing that the few seconds it takes will never get in the way of making their class on time, but it'll make a big difference in how well they'll be able to ride it.

Here are a few more examples of stress-stoppers. A rider:

- Always shows wearing the same britches and lucky belt.

- Always shows with her shirt just a tiny bit untucked.

- Picks up her horse's hoof and rubs the horseshoe for a little good luck.

- Braids her horse's mane at the withers (while in the saddle) to stay relaxed.

- Draws a heart on the horse's neck with her finger when feeling pressure.

Rub here for good luck!

- Rides with her tongue hanging out of the side of her mouth.

- Kisses her horse on the nose, hugs his neck, smells his body, or rubs his soft ears to calm her down when feeling pressure.

 How to Create **Effective Stress-Stoppers**

1 Use them at the same *time*—every time—when arriving at the show grounds, upon hearing the bell in dressage, or just prior to mounting, for example.

2 Use them at the same *location*—every time—when you enter the arena or walk into the cross-country start box, for example. Using them at the *same time* and in the *same location* makes them *predictable,* something that's very important when it comes to stopping the effect stress can have on you.

3 Make your stress-stopper as *repeatable* as possible. For instance, if your *stress-stopper* is to eat a taco each time you get nervous, you could be in trouble when there aren't any Mexican restaurants at the show grounds!

4 Whenever possible make your *stress-stoppers* "touchable." Rubbing the horseshoe for good luck, rubbing your horse's ear, or pushing the imaginary stop button on your horse's nose are three examples of touchable stress-stoppers.

Pressure Proof Plan **Stress-Stopper**

Write down your *stress-stopper*:

_____

_____

Write down when or where you'll use it:

_____

_____

2 Toughness Training

Another technique that can help you *gain*, *maintain*, or *regain* mental control is something called *toughness training*. "When the going gets tough, the tough get going," and "It's not the size of the dog in the fight but the size of the fight in the dog," are two phrases that speak to the value of mental toughness. It's important to remember that this is not the same kind of toughness you see in sports like football and hockey where aggression and intimidation are rewarded. The kind of toughness you need to develop is the kind that allows you to remain mentally strong in the face of adversity, believe in yourself even after making a mistake, and never give up regardless of the challenge.

Make the rest of your ride the best of your ride.

While *toughness training* is a tool taught to all elite athletes, it was actually developed in Hollywood. Also called *tough acting*, movie stars use it to get into character or create a specific emotion for film. Some actors are so good at *tough acting* that they can actually think sad thoughts and cry for the camera (once again, proving that emotions really do affect our motions). This technique has also been called *fake it till you make it* (even though the actor isn't really sad, he fakes it by thinking sad thoughts, recalling sad memories, frowning, and hunching his shoulders). Actors can *fake* sadness until they *make* sadness.

I'm Calm, Cool, and Collected.

Just like an actor, you can also use *tough acting.* However, instead of creating *sad motions* that lead to *sad emotions*, you purposely create *confident motions* so they can lead to *confident emotions.* For example, if you're feeling doubt, you can fake confidence by standing up tall; smiling; opening your shoulders; thinking positive thoughts; and walking and talking in a confident manner. Likewise, if you want to pump yourself up, you can jump up and down and shake your shoulders, and if you want to calm yourself down, you can walk and talk in slow motion. If you want to create an emotion on the *inside*, start by *faking* it on the *outside*. And as mentioned, the opposite is also

Fake it until you make it.

Riding can be tough. But so can you.

true: Creating positive and confident emotions on the *inside* can also help you develop positive and confident motions on the *outside*.

tip How to Create Your Toughness-Training Program

There are three things you need:

1 Dress Respect—Purposely dress nicely knowing that when you look good, you feel good, and when you feel good, you often perform well. This is why Olympic teams wear uniforms for the Opening Ceremonies: If they were allowed to parade in their pajamas they might have a difficult time getting motivated for the demands of the competition the next day.

2 A Strong Self—Always learn to keep your problems to yourself. Even when you're feeling tired and have a headache, keep it to yourself instead of telling everyone. There are only two reasons for telling others and neither are very confident: You're either looking for sympathy or you're establishing a *pre-excuse* in case things don't go well. To become a confident rider you need to believe in your ability to succeed rather than have excuses prepared in case you don't.

3 A Toughness Trigger—Create a predefined *movement* and repeat it each time you experience stress. When done correctly, the movement will remind you that you have the ability to overcome. For example, if you're afraid of falling, mimic the movement of putting on a seat belt; once you're snapped in tight you can take a deep breath, knowing that you're nice and secure. In this example, the motion of putting on the seatbelt is your *trigger* to be *tough*. The best *toughness trigger* is the one that can be accomplished without letting go of the reins. Here are a few good examples:

- A rider distracted by an argument with her husband can mimic the motion of hanging up the phone (she'll call him back later when she's finished riding).

- A young rider distracted by an important math test tomorrow can mimic the motion of closing a book (she'll study later when she gets home).

- A rider doubting her ability can stick both thumbs in the air while riding as if to say, "I'm fine, two thumbs up."

- A rider facing a challenge can blink and hold her eyes closed for a split second. When she opens them again she reminds herself to see everything in a new light.

- After listening to a trash-talker, a rider can mimic the motion of throwing something into the trash can (the trash is the negativity from the trash-talker).

Pressure Proof Plan **Toughness Training**

Write down how you'll fake confidence:

_____

_____

Write down a *toughness trigger*:

_____

_____

Write down when you'll use them:

_____

_____

3 Desensitization

Sooner or later you're going to encounter a stressful situation, but it's not the situation itself that will limit your ability—it's how you react to it. Many riders simply try and avoid stressful situations, believing that avoiding them will make everything feel better. While it might be true in the short term, avoiding challenges simply holds you back from overcoming them.

Desensitization is the opposite of avoidance. Instead of avoiding a challenge, you welcome it and repeat it, knowing that the more you experience it, the more likely you'll begin to feel capable of controlling it. For example, if you get nervous showing in front of crowds, you can either schedule all your lessons when no one's around (avoidance) or schedule them when lots of people are watching (knowing that the more you experience crowds the better chance you'll have of desensitizing yourself to the stress associated with them). It might take a little time, but it'll be well worth it. In the end, desensitization helps you to become

"Tell everyone to stop watching..."

Comfortable and Uncomfortable

In order to desensitize yourself to stressors like riding in front of crowds you're going to need to get comfortable (by doing it all the time) at being uncomfortable (riding in front of crowds) until it becomes comfortable (you've experienced it so much that it no longer bothers you).

Pressure Proof by identifying challenges and purposely exposing yourself to them.

Desensitization vs. Imprinting

Desensitization is a valuable tool for both horse and rider. If you want an adult horse to stand quietly for the farrier; be easy to groom; work well with children; and develop into a confident competitor, you tap his hooves with a hammer; clip him; caress his ears; and separate him from his stall mates from time to time when he's baby. If he experiences these things on a regular basis, the stress associated with them will lessen.

Get comfortable at being uncomfortable until it becomes comfortable.

Avoid them, however, and the stress can linger for a lifetime. This is called *imprinting* and there's one small difference between it and desensitization. *Imprinting* is the term used when you have no past experience with a stressor (the first time you go to a horse show), while *desensitization* occurs when you have had previous experience with the stressor (when a first horse show doesn't go well and you dread going to the second one).

I'm desensitizing him to me!

The first step in any *desensitization* or *imprinting* program is to define how you should act when you encounter a stressor. Taking a few deep breaths; recalling a positive *memory motivation* from your past; *targeting* your focus onto the sound of your horse's hooves; and repeating a *motivating motto* are a few good ideas. Once you've decided how you'll act, you select the kind of desensitization that best suits your situation and get started.

Kinds of Desensitization

- **Systemic**—Gradually desensitize yourself to a stressor, step by step. For instance, if jumping makes you nervous, start by (1) trotting ground poles, (2) trotting cross-rails, (3) cantering ground poles, (4) cantering cross-rails, (5) trotting small verticals, and finally, (6) cantering small verticals.

- **Immersion**—Desensitize yourself by immersing yourself in it, mentally and physically. For instance, if showing in crowds makes you nervous, (1) visualize yourself showing well in front of a crowd, (2) change your private lessons to group, (3) imagine your favorite rider showing in a crowd, and (4) show in front of a small crowd followed by a large one.

- **Flooding**—Desensitize yourself to a stressor by doing it all at once, over and over. For instance, if moving up from a pony to a horse makes you nervous, have the courage to ride the horse many times without trying to buy another pony! It's hard, but it's worth it.

- **Bio-Desensitization**—Desensitize yourself using *biofeedback*. Start by visualizing a stressor while purposefully creating the kind of reactions normally associated with it (like holding your breath and clenching your fists). Once you feel them, use a relaxation technique like a *deep breath* and a *calming motto* and *memory* to relax. The next time stress causes you to feel these things, recall how you solved it and do it again for real.

You can desensitize or imprint yourself against almost any mental or physical stressors. For example, a trainer once imprinted her young students to the fear of falling by pushing each of them off the top of a pony. The first rider mounted, sat as happy as can be and then, boom, down she went. Without missing a beat, the next little girl mounted up and seconds

later she was on the ground, too. For 30 minutes their parents watched in horror thinking, "I don't think she likes children very much," as the trainer pushed them all off the pony.

Afterward the trainer told the parents that beginners often have a fear of falling so in their first lesson ever, she makes them so good at it that it doesn't bother them anymore. She then continued by saying that after 15 minutes of falling they all figure out how to land on their feet, and after 30 minutes, she no longer even needs to push—they mount up and throw themselves off!

She summarized saying that by the end of the lesson they learn their emergency dismount, overcome their fear of falling, and are now able to get on with it: they can learn the posting-trot diagonals without wondering what it's going to feel like to fall from the top of a horse because they've repeated it so much they're now desensitized to the fear of falling.

Pressure Proof Plan **Desensitization**

Write down something that makes you nervous:

_____

_____

Write down a plan to overcome it:

_____

_____

4 Targeting

Also called *object help, targeting* helps draw your focus away from stressful challenges by purposely placing it on positive *objects*. In the movie *Cast Away* with Tom Hanks playing a man alone on an island, a volleyball took Hanks' attention away from being lonely: The volleyball became the *object* that *helped* him cope with stress. All athletes can use *targeting*: Marathon runners are taught to focus on one telephone pole at a time to avoid thinking of the vastness of their race, and basketball players are taught to focus on the small rings that attach the net to the hoop to avoid *overthinking* a shot.

When it comes to riding, however, *targeting* must work differently because you can't allow yourself to focus on surrounding objects when you're in the saddle. You don't have the luxury of staring at telephone poles nor can you carry a volleyball with you. Instead, you train yourself to focus on positive *targets* like calm *sensations* and *sounds*. For instance, when feeling nervous, you can take a deep breath and focus on:

- **Sensations** such as the feeling of the stitching on your reins, the rhythm of the canter, or the beating of your heart.

- **Sounds** like the noise your horse's hooves make when they contact the ground, the sound your horse makes when he breathes (especially if he's a blower), or the sound of the wind.

Another interesting way to use *object help* is to write a list of distractions (like the argument you're having with your husband or the math test you're

Skittles

Young riders used to complain about having to ride a school horse named "Buckshot Devil." That all changed the day the trainer changed the horse's name to "Skittles" and hung a glittery pink nametag on her door. Afterward, everyone lined up to ride her because the trainer had *reframed* her as something kind and sweet, rather than something devilish.

worried about) and then file this list away by locking it in your tack trunk until you finish riding (you can think about those things but only after you've dismounted). In this example, the tack trunk becomes the *object* that *helps* you focus on your riding.

Reframing

Another interesting form of targeting is called *reframing*. In this technique, you *reframe* stressors and fears into thoughts or objects that are more pleasant and less intimidating. Perhaps the most common example of reframing is a nervous public speaker imagining his audience members wearing only their underwear. If he can do this, the stress of the situation just seems more manageable. One way a rider can do it is by calling the scariest fence on course the "big purple thingy with the flowered sticky-thing poking out," or imagining the dressage judge as a great personal friend. Regardless of the stressor, there's always a way to *reframe* it so that it seems less intimidating.

"Here comes the big purple thing with the little flowered stick things poking out."

Pressure Proof Plan **Targeting**

Write down something that makes you feel stressed:

_____

_____

Write down an *object* that can help:

_____

Write down a way to *reframe* this stressor:

_____

_____

4 Relaxation Techniques

Anxiety affects all of us in different ways, but most of these ways are quite detrimental to our performance. When your level of arousal becomes too high you need to be able to get it under control. One of the most effective ways to do this is through the use of a *relaxation technique*. There are many different types: The most common is called *progressive relaxation*, alternating between tensing and relaxing a muscle.

Progressive Relaxation

The idea behind *progressive relaxation* is that a muscle is able to reach a deeper level of relaxation and suppleness immediately after being contracted. The word *progressive* means that you start by contracting and relaxing one muscle group at a time then *progressively* move through every major muscle group in your body until each one has been contracted and relaxed.

While *progressive relaxation* is very successful it does have a few drawbacks. First of all it can take up to 30 minutes to progressively contract and relax every muscle group in your body (sometimes you just don't have that much time to calm down). The second drawback is that it can often relax you to the point where you're *too* calm—remember that effective riding requires some degree of excitement, energy, and engagement. When you're too relaxed your butterflies fly away and you risk feeling lethargic or unmotivated. Luckily, there are a few variations of *progressive relaxation* that are less time-consuming and perhaps more appropriate when it comes to creating the correct amount of arousal.

There are five forms of *progressive relaxation:*

"I think I overdid my relaxation exercises..."

1 Full Body—You progressively contract and relax your muscles in a predefined order to achieve deep relaxation. This form is best when used to ensure a good night's sleep before a show; while recovering from injury; or during a rest period throughout the season.

2 Relaxation Phase Only—Similar to the *full body*, this time you skip the muscle contraction phase and only do the relaxation phase. Most riders find this more successful because it helps them achieve a good deal of relaxation in a limited amount of time—usually less than 15 minutes.

3 Combined Muscle Group—Similar to the *relaxation phase*, but instead of relaxing individual muscles like the biceps and triceps, you relax the entire arm. This technique is also great for riders because it usually takes less than 5 minutes to complete.

4 Complete Phase—Similar to the *combined muscle group*, instead of relaxing a body part, you relax your entire body all at the same time. You won't be able to reach as deep a level of relaxation as the other techniques, but it works well on competition day because it only takes a few seconds to complete.

5 Deep Breathing Phase—Instead of relaxing your muscles, you simply take a long, slow, deep, diaphragmatic breath and relax your entire body as you exhale. This technique only takes a few seconds and works best during competition when you need to focus or recover after a mistake.

Differential Relaxation

Another relaxation technique—one that's perhaps even better suited to riding—is called *differential relaxation*. Unlike *progressive relaxation*, when doing *differential relaxation* you relax some muscles while simultaneously contracting others. The idea behind this is that you need to ask different things of different parts of your body. For example, in the jumping position you contract your back and core muscles to create a good position while simultaneously relaxing your elbows so that your hands can follow the movement of your horse (the release).

Consequently, learning to relax your entire body through *progressive relaxation* may not be the best way to prepare for this kind of action. Instead, *differential relaxation* encourages you to learn to quickly and purposely alternate between relaxing and contracting different muscle groups simultaneously. When you do this, you achieve a more appropriate level of muscle *relaxation* and *engagement* while ensuring muscles continue to work in a supple yet athletic and purposeful way (you can't ride well when a muscle that should be supple is contracted, or when a muscle that should be contracted is supple).

tip   How to Feel **Differential Relaxation**

To better understand how *differential relaxation* works try this simple test:

1 In a seated position, place your right forearm on top of your right thigh so that your index finger is resting on your knee. To start, completely relax all the muscles of your forearm, hand, and fingers and then tap your index finger as many times on your knee as you can in 10 seconds. Remember to keep the muscles of your hand completely relaxed and free of tension.

2 Take a short break and then repeat the test again, only this time contract and tighten every muscle in your forearm, hand, and fingers.

3 For the final part of the test, relax all the muscles of your hand and fingers while simultaneously contracting the muscles of your forearm.

So how did you do? Chances are good that you achieved the greatest success in the final test when your muscles were *differentially relaxed*, when one group was *purposely relaxed* while the other was *purposely contracted*.

Energizing Techniques

Relaxation techniques work wonders when you want to calm yourself down, but they are not appropriate when you need to pump yourself up—that's when you need *energizing techniques* instead. Listening to *motivating music*, visualizing a *powerful memory* from your past, and jumping up and down briskly are a few easy ways to increase your level of energy.

6 Deep Breathing

There are many different *stress-management techniques,* but regardless of the ones you use, you should always remember to match them with a few deep breaths. When the stress of a situation becomes too great, it's often common to put some important things on momentary hold. While this makes pretty good sense it does get a bit weird when one of the things you decide to put on hold is breathing! We've all done it: Whether caused by a scary movie or bad news (or a scary or bad horse!) many of us hold our breath as a response to stress. Since this makes you become tight and tense you must remember to breathe when it counts the most.

"If you're feeling blue, BREATHE!"

In the presence of stress many chemical, biological, and neurological changes occur in your brain that prepares it for the *fight or flight* (and in severe cases, *freeze*) *reflex.* One of the first things to occur in your body is an acceleration of your heart rate, ensuring you're physically prepared to either *fight* against the stress, or *flee* from it, and when the speed of your heart is increased, the rest of your body speeds up, too. This is why so many riders tend to rush their fences, collapse their corners, and walk, talk, and react too quickly when feeling pressure.

Unfortunately, when stress causes your heart rate to increase, your performance decreases. When stress alone (*not* exercise) causes your heart rate to reach 120 beats per minute (bpm), your mind and body begin to lose their sharpness and control. At 140 bpm, you lose your ability to repeat learned skills, and when you reach 150 bpm, your mind basically begins to shut down. In this state, even the best riders lose their ability to maintain mental and physical focus.

So what can you do to make sure that you avoid this unwanted speeding up of your mind and body? In a word, *breathe*. Inhaling air deep into your lungs has been proven to change the biology of your body in such a way that it actually slows your heart rate—and when you slow your heart rate you can slow the rest of your body, too. When you're able to do this you can avoid much of the rushing and pressure that's so often associated with stress.

Diaphragmatic Breathing

You're going to breath over 17,000 times today, and your heart will beat over 100,000 times. If you're going to do something this much, you might as well make sure you're doing it well. Not all breathing is created equal; *diaphragmatic* breathing (as compared to *chest* breathing) is considered the most effective method of breathing.

You can train yourself to take *diaphragmatic* breaths by inhaling air through your nose and filling the bottom part of your lungs by pushing your diaphragm down and your stomach out. Next, fill the middle portion

 tip How to Tell if You're a **Diaphragm Breather**

1 Place one hand on your stomach and the other on your chest.

2 Inhale deeply.

3 If the hand on your stomach moves out, you're a *diaphragm* breather. If the hand on your chest moves up, you're a *chest* breather.

4 Exhale.

5 If the hand on your stomach moves in, you're a *diaphragm* breather. If the hand on your chest moves down, you're a *chest* breather (the hand on your chest should not move very much).

of your lungs by expanding your chest and raising your rib cage. Lastly, fill the top part of your lungs by slightly raising your chest and shoulders. Then, slowly exhale through the mouth emptying your lungs from the top down while feeling the tension leave your body along with the expelled air.

Ratio and Centered Breathing

When *diaphragmatic breathing* becomes second nature you can begin to create different variations of it. The first is called *ratio breathing,* exhaling for twice as long as you inhale (a 1:2 ratio)—for example, inhaling for four seconds and exhaling for eight seconds.

A second variation—often called *centered breathing*—adds another number to the ratio, such as 4:2:8, which means, inhaling for four seconds, *holding* your breath for two, then exhaling for eight. During the slight "breath-holding" phase, relax and attempt to get in touch with the sensations occurring within your body (become "centered"). Both variations stretch your breaths to between 12 to 14 seconds—something that's necessary to ensure sufficient oxygen is being inhaled to slow your heart rate.

Plan your ride and ride your plan.

Young riders can also use *ratio* and *centered* breathing but should change the duration to 3:2:5. Matching your deep breaths to *calming words, memories,* or *mottos* can create an even greater level of relaxation and help you develop the feeling of being "centered."

Slow *ratio* and *centered* breathing can help you to relax, but are they appropriate for times when you need to get pumped up? At these times, you should actually consider increasing the speed of your ratio from a 4:2:8 to something quicker like 2:1:3. When you speed up the rate of your breathing, you speed up the energy in your body. You just need to remember to limit this kind of breathing so that you don't become overly excited or anxious. When breathing is being used as a tool to create excitement and

"I think I'm hyperventilating!"

energy, always limit it to no more than three or four cycles; if you do any more you may begin to hyperventilate.

While breathing is an automatic reflex, *diaphragmatic breathing* does require some effort. In the beginning, you should practice it several times a day for a week before incorporating it into your riding lessons. As soon as you're comfortable with it at home, practice it in your schooling sessions. Once you're capable of doing it when schooling, challenge yourself by increasing or decreasing the pressure of your lessons so that your heart rate increases or decreases (when you feel it happening, start your breathing exercises and prove that you can control your mind and body). This is a form of *biofeedback*: sensing changes in your body and then eliciting the necessary action to regain control of those changes. As soon as you master *diaphragmatic, ratio,* and *centered* breathing while schooling, you're ready to give it a try while showing.

7 Pre-Competition Routines

Stress might seem to affect you most on show days, but it doesn't always start then. In fact, most stress actually starts several days earlier—the anticipation and worry surrounding a competition or stressful event can plant a seed of doubt in your mind that grows as it approaches. One way to overcome this is to create a *step-by-step* plan well in advance so that you can maintain the perception of control. This plan is called a *pre-competition routine.*

A *pre-competition routine* is a set of predefined and timely behaviors that help you create a sense of control before a potentially stressful event. It can include things like checking your horse's shoes four days before a show; packing your tack trunk the day before; longeing your horse a few hours before; and drinking a sports drink a few minutes before. If you're able to create a predictable routine like this you can develop the perception of control. You may not be able to control everything that happens at the show (the weather and delays, for example) but you can certainly control what happens to you as you prepare for it. This can be especially helpful when you repeat the same *pre-competition routine* before every show because it can provide you with a sense of predictability and controllability that is so important to feeling *Pressure Proof*.

You can't always <u>predict</u> but you can always <u>prepare</u>.

Present and Performer Mindset

Before you can create your *pre-competition routine* you need to identify what should be included. To do this you must first identify two important mindsets:

1 Present Mindset—The rider you are at this very second. For example, let's say you're currently tired, hungry, and thirsty.

2 Performer Mindset—The rider you must be in order to perform your best. Using the example above, you'll need to begin getting plenty of rest, eating well, and hydrating before you're able to ride or compete at your best.

Identifying the differences between your *present* and *performer* selves helps you identify exactly what should be included in your *pre-competition routine*. It should consist of *mental* skills, such as memorizing your dressage test; familiarizing yourself with the driving directions to the venue; knowing where the warm-up arenas are; and identifying a *motivating song* to use on show day.

It should also consist of *physical* skills like preparing the correct studs; checking your tack; packing your tack trunk; locating your medical arm band; and longeing your horse the day before. Lastly, it should also include *behavioral* skills including the following:

"I was told to bank rest today!"

- **"Bank" Rest**—The hours spent hauling, sleeping in trailers, and driving to hotels, along with lots of early morning competition can make it difficult for you to get a normal amount of sleep on show weekends. To battle the toll that insufficient rest can take on you, *bank rest* by purposely getting a few extra hours of rest the week *before* the show to make up for what you'll likely lose *at* the show. Listening to calm music; taking a 15-minute catnap in the middle of the day; stopping strenuous exercise three hours before bedtime; and going to bed the same time each night are good ways to help.

- **Nutrition**—You are what you eat—to ride well you must eat well. Eat a healthy diet of several small meals each day (called *grazing*) and you'll provide your body with a constant flow of the nutrition and energy needed to ride well and maintain an active metabolism. Overeating interferes with your ability to ride well, and poor eating habits interfere with your ability to provide your mind and body with the best form of fuel. Planning in advance by packing a few healthy meals means you can avoid stopping for potato chips at every service station between your home and the show.

- **Hydration**—Water makes up 75 percent of your body and 74 percent of your brain; without it neither can function at its best. Most of us drink when we're thirsty, but being thirsty means we're already dehydrated (you need to drink *before* you feel thirsty). Your physical performance starts to drop when you're only 2 percent dehydrated (you can die when you're 4 percent dehydrated). On average, 65 to 80 percent of us are currently dehydrated. To find out how much water you should drink each day simply divide your body weight in pounds by two; the result is the minimum number of fluid ounces you need (more if you exercise or ride in a hot climate). The best fluids are those that are clear and use things like lemon, ginger, or strawberry instead of sweeteners to add flavor. Even veggies and fruit can help you meet your daily requirement of fluids.

To Eat or Not

The next time you reach for snack, ask yourself, "Am I hungry enough to eat an apple?" When the answer is no, you're not really hungry, you just have the "munchies."

Lucky Seven Routine

A great way to set and manage your *pre-competition routine* is to divide it into three different time periods:

- **7 days** to 1 day before a show (the week before an important ride).

- **7 hours** to 1 hour before (the day of the show).

- **7 minutes** to 1 minute before (mounted and ready to go).

During each phase you should give yourself a variety of different tasks to complete. This is a great way of making your *pre-competition routine* predictable, controllable, and manageable. Here are good examples:

7 Days to 1 Day Before a Big Show

- **7 days before**—Start *banking rest* using a *relaxation technique* (p. 209).

- **6 days before**—Write down your goals for the upcoming show (p. 176).

- **5 days before**—Print the driving directions to the venue and confirm your entries.

- **4 days before**—Check to see that your horse's shoes are in good condition.

- **3 days before**—Eliminate all junk food and start hydrating.

- **2 days before**—Pack your tack trunk using a checklist so nothing gets forgotten.

- **1 day before**—Take your horse for a light hack on this day off.

7 Hours to 1 Hour Before a Big Show

- **7 hours before**—Recall your *positive memory motivation* (p. 160).

- **6 hours before**—Review your *short-* and *long-term* goals for the show (p. 170).

- **5 hours before**—Repeat (out loud) your positive *self-image statement* (p. 130).

- **4 hours before**—Check all your tack and confirm the location of your riding arenas.

- **3 hours before**—Start listening to your *motivating music* (p. 133).

- **2 hours before**—Start visualizing your *riding rehearsals* (p. 145).

- **1 hour before**—Reconfirm your entries, start times, and arena locations.

7 Minutes to 1 Minute Before a Big Show

- **7 minutes before**—Repeat your positive *cue word* several times (p. 115).

- **6 minutes before**—Sing out loud the *motivating message* from your song (p. 135).

- **5 minutes before**—Continue visualizing your *riding rehearsals* (p. 145).

- **4 minutes before**—Repeat your positive "C" *emotions* and <u>A</u>lways <u>B</u>e your "<u>C</u>s" (p. 125).

- **3 minutes before**—Ask yourself a *leading question* and answer it in a positive way (p. 121).

- **2 minutes before**—Repeat out loud your *motivating motto* several times (p. 128).

- **1 minute before**—Take a few *deep breaths,* visualize your *riding rehearsal,* and recall your *motivating memory* one last time, then say your *motivating motto, cue word,* "C" *emotions,* and *self-image statement* out loud.

If you can establish (and repeat) a purposeful and predictable plan like this you stand a great chance of feeling well prepared for whatever comes your way, both physically and mentally. This is what being *Pressure Proof* is all about. This is the purpose of the *pre-competition routine*—developing a series of positive actions that will allow you to control your emotions before an important ride, rather than approaching the event in a random way that might ultimately leave you feeling like your emotions are taking control of you.

Pressure Proof Plan **Pre-Competition Routine**

Write down what you'll do 7 days to 1 day before an important ride:

(7) _____   (3) _____

(6) _____   (2) _____

(5) _____   (1) _____

(4) _____

Write down what you'll do 7 hours to 1 hour before an important ride:

(7) _____   (3) _____

(6) _____   (2) _____

(5) _____   (1) _____

(4) _____

Write down what you'll do 7 minutes to 1 minute before an important ride:

(7) _____   (3) _____

(6) _____   (2) _____

(5) _____   (1) _____

(4) _____

PRESSURE PROOF PROJECT

Rate Your Stress-Management Skills

Answer the following questions to determine if *stress management* can help you improve your riding:

0 = Never   1 = Sometimes   2 = Almost Always

_____ I *control and manage stress* instead of trying to eliminate stressful situations.

_____ When schooling and showing I always feel *aroused*, not anxious or apathetic.

_____ I act as if I feel *confident* even when I'm not feeling confident (I fake it until I make it).

_____ I *desensitize* myself to stressors by re-creating and practicing (not avoiding) them.

_____ I use a *relaxation technique* to help me rest or stay calm when I'm feeling pressured.

_____ I use an *energizing technique* to pump me up when I'm feeling unmotivated.

_____ I use a *stress-stopper* (superstition, ritual) to maintain the perception of control.

_____ I use *deep breathing* to control my level of anxiety.

_____ I know who I must become to ride my best (*present* vs. *performer* self).

_____ I use a *pre-competition routine* (checklist) to maintain the perception of control.

_____ **Total** (add up your answers).

If your score added up to:

14 to 20
Great—you've learned the value of stress management and can use it effectively. There's always room for improvement so continue to think about what you read in this chapter.

8 to 13
You're on the right track but need more training to help you deal with stress. Make a list of the challenges that bother you the most and start improving them by using the tools in this chapter.

0 to 7
Stress has too much effect on you. You need a mental-training program to help you cope, not mope. Read this chapter again very carefully and create a stress-management plan that will help you.

9

Remembering
It All

There's nothing <u>wrong</u> with you that can't be corrected with what's <u>right</u> with you.

Get It Together and Keep It Together

Many riders agree that it's often easy to *get* it together but sometimes pretty hard to *keep* it together. Everything feels fine in the beginning but when the pressure goes up, they struggle under its weight. Perhaps one of the biggest differences between good riders and great riders is that the great ones don't just *get* it together, they *keep* it together. They do this by dedicating themselves to their mental-training program as much as they do to their physical-training program. They never give up when things get tough and they are willing to keep working at it even when they make a mistake or when the rewards are not immediate. Like learning a new language, these riders know that mental training can be challenging in the beginning, but with a little time and effort, their skills will soon become fluent. Unlike a rider with a short attention span or the need for immediate reward, *Pressure Proof* riders are in it for the long term.

It's been said that achieving greatness in anything can take up to 10 years or 10,000 hours of training. While the exact number will obviously vary from rider to rider, it's important to remember that anything worth achieving is worth working and waiting for. One thing that can make this a bit challenging is simply finding the time to work on it. Commitments like work, school, and family can monopolize so much of your time that it can be difficult to imagine adding anything more to the pile. The good news is that even five or 10 minutes a day can prove very beneficial. All you need to do is be creative in finding this time.

tip — How to Find Time for **Pressure Proof** Workouts

Mental Multi-Tasking—Work on your mental exercises while actually riding. For example, you can come up with a *motivating motto* while going for a hack, or find *motivating music* for your pre-competition playlist by listening to music while driving to a lesson. You can also work on these exercises when you are grooming; working on the ground; exercising; warming up; cooling down; or stretching.

Time Blocking—Wear an imaginary "Do Not Disturb" sign and block a certain amount of time each day to focus on your mental exercises.

"Honey Do" List—Make a list of the daily and weekly mental exercises you want to complete. Then stick with this schedule and treat it like any other important commitment in your calendar.

"Honey Don't" List—Make a list of the things that waste your time, and then avoid doing them. Time spent watching TV or talking to *trash-talkers* could be much better spent.

Batch List—Batch your daily chores together so that you can create a little extra time to work on your mental exercises. For example, cleaning your tack while discussing next week's lesson plan with your trainer means you can work on your mental exercises when you'd normally be cleaning your tack.

Honey Don't List
1. Don't watch too much TV
2. Don't talk to trash talkers
3. Don't waste time worrying
4. Don't skip lessons
5. Don't give up!

Time for 10—Ask yourself, "What could I do if I had an extra 10 minutes each day?" If your answer is to get in shape then take 10 minutes to walk up the stairs instead of taking the elevator. If it's to find a *motivating song* then wake up 10 minutes earlier and listen to music. If you look for these 10 minutes a day, there's a good chance you'll find them. In the end, they can add an extra four or five hours to each month for your mental-training program.

Take the time to make the time.

It's been said that the four words that most characterize mediocrity are "I don't have time." We need to remind ourselves that we *do* have the time; we just need to use our time to its fullest. There are 1,440 minutes a day, 168 hours a week, 720 hours a month, or 8,640 hours a year. You just need to be willing to dedicate some of them to your mental exercises. The good news is that you don't need to dedicate every day of your life to it—new habits are formed in as few as 21 days—so instead of burdening yourself with the idea of working hard on mental training forever, simply set a goal to work hard on it for the next three weeks.

This is the same principle behind positive *lifestyle* changes such as joining a gym or stopping smoking; if you do it well for three weeks, you won't have to work at it anymore because it will have become a habit.

Pressure Proof **Your Memory**

1 **Memory**

There are many effective tools and techniques in this book but they won't help you much if you can't remember them. Our brains can store up to 100 trillion bits of information so why is it we forget what we heard yesterday or can't remember our dressage test or jump course? Unfortunately, memory likes to play tricks: It recalls things we've never tried to remember (like a song lyric learned in childhood) but forgets important things we just learned. Sometimes it seems that we remember what we want to forget, and forget what we want to remember!

"Do Point": The moment you decide to focus on what you <u>can</u> do rather than on what you <u>can't</u>.

There are three main reasons we forget something: We didn't get it to begin with; we had it but lost it; or we had it but can't seem to find it. These frustrating problems indicate a breakdown in one of three important areas of memory.

The first is how you take information in and how you feel about it. This is called *encoding* and is required for the development of long-term memory. For example, if you're sure you'll forget your dressage test there's a pretty good chance you will.

The second breakdown occurs in your *storage* capacity. For example, if you're trying to remember three different jumping courses at the same time there's a good chance you'll forget one because you don't have enough room to store all three.

The third area is in your *retrieval* area. This is often called the "on-the-tip-of-my-tongue" syndrome. For example, you've walked the cross-country course but when riding it you just can't seem to remember if the next fence is a log or a ditch.

Sensory, Short-Term, and Long-Term Memory

There are many different kinds of memory, some lasting longer than others. The shortest of all is called *sensory memory* and it only lasts for a few seconds. For instance, if you hear (called an *echo*) or see (called an *icon*) a list of words for a split second, you'll only be able to remember a maximum of four of them because you'll forget the rest of the list by the time you say the first four words.

"I can't remember if I lost my horse or found this halter..."

The second kind of memory, called *short-term memory,* (often called *working* memory) lasts a little longer but is still limited to about 20 seconds. It preserves recent experiences but is only able to hold five and nine pieces of information at a time. A phone number is a good example; if you hear it once you probably won't remember it because it has too many digits.

The last form of memory is called *long-term* memory and this is where all your life experiences, events, facts, emotions, and skills are stored for a long period of time.

When was the last time you did something for the first time?

To increase the likelihood of remembering important facts, you need to train yourself to *encode* the information in a meaningful and productive way. If you can do this, you can transfer some of your *sensory* and *short-term* memories to your *long-term* memory.

tip How to Transfer **Sensory** and **Short-Term Memories** to **Long-Term Memory**

Use Mnemonic Devices—Associating information with familiar and stimulating wordplay including *acronyms* (like your *cue words*); *alliteration* (like your positive "C" emotions); *rhyme* (like the *motto,* "If it's going to be, it's up to me"); and *language mediators,* like creating a sentence to link things together (for example, "All King Edward's Horses Can Manage Big Fences" is a great way to remember the letters in a small dressage arena). When it comes to wordplay, your brain prefers positive to negative, humorous to normal, and vivid to dull. The more interesting and stimulating the input, the greater chance you'll have of remembering it.

Create Mental Imagery—This is an essential part of building long-term memory because thinking in *mental images* engages the left and right sides of your brain. For example, when you run into an acquaintance, your right brain recalls her face while your left brain remembers her name.

Another *visualization technique* called *loci* helps *encode* information by imagining things in their place. For instance, if you're at the store and have forgotten your shopping list, imagine what the list looked like when you were at home. Likewise, if you know you've forgotten a piece of tack, visually imagine all your tack in its place in the tack trunk in order to identify which piece is missing.

Riding rehearsals are yet another great example of how *mental imagery* can help you remember something important like a dressage test or a jumping course.

"Did anyone see my rider?"

Repeat, Repeat, and Repeat—This is an almost mandatory stage in the development of long-term memory. For instance, repeating a person's name three times in the first conversation with him; or repeating (out loud) a phone number each time you dial it are just two ways to make sure the information sticks. Just like walking between your home and your barn over and over again will create a path in the ground, repeating something over and over in your mind will create a path between it and your memories.

Input Correctly—The way you put information in has a lot to do with how easily you'll get it out. It's like studying for a multiple-choice test and then discovering that it's actually an essay test. You're not in trouble because you don't know the information, you're in trouble because you put it in wrong. Memorizing a dressage test by mentally rehearsing it in your mind is a good example of putting the information in correctly.

The "Write to Remember": Write it if you want to remember it!

2 Making It Work

Many mental tools can help you match your strong body with an equally strong mind. *Music motivation, cue words, riding rehearsals,* and *stress-stoppers* are just a few. As I mentioned before, however, they can only help you if you remember to use them. This means that the only thing more important than the tools themselves is your ability to remember them. The next several pages will help you do this.

How to Remember Your Mental Tools

1 Pick Your Top Three—The first time you learn a list of items you're only able to remember five to nine of them, so expecting yourself to remember every single tool in this book is unreasonable. The first thing you should do, therefore, is simply select your three favorites and work with them only (for now). Once you've selected your "Top Three," you can move on to the next tip.

2 Start Early—If you're so nervous on Wednesday you can't sleep; so tense on Thursday you can't eat; and so worried on Friday you develop the world's biggest case of self-doubt, diarrhea, and dry heaves (more bad "D" words!) chances are pretty good your Top Three might not be able to help you when you arrive at the show grounds on Saturday morning. Show jitters and pressure sets in well before a stressful event so you need to start using your Top Three early. For example, you can repeat your *cue word* all day Wednesday; relive your *memory motivation* all day Thursday; and imagine your *riding rehearsals* all day Friday. On Saturday morning, repeat all three while listening to your favorite *motivating music* and taking a few *deep breaths*. By starting early, you can learn to take control of your emotions before they start taking control of you!

3 Use Concentration Cues—To ensure that your "Top Three" become memorable you're going to need to think of them often. One way you can do this is to *link* them to things that occur often in your life. For example, if you can't stop thinking of a bad fall, tell yourself to think of a positive riding memory every time you open a door (the door becomes your *cue* to *concentrate* on the positive memory). You can open hundreds of doors each day: to enter the office; to leave it; to enter the bathroom; to go into the stall; to exit the stall; to leave the bathroom; and finally another one to re-enter your office (seven doors in five minutes)! Another example is to write the letters "MM" on your watch: Whenever you look at the time you'll be reminded to think of a positive memory (the "MM" on your watch stands for *Memory Motivation*). If you get in the habit of thinking positive memories each time you open a door or look at your watch, they'll start to become automatic.

Concentration cues can be:

- **Sounds,** like the ding of the bell before you enter the dressage arena, or the sound of your class being called over the show ground's PA system.

- **Locations,** like the start box on cross-country or the letter "C" in dressage.

- **Movements** of your body, like putting on your boots or snapping the harness on your helmet.

For example, a dressage rider can motivate herself by singing her *motivating song* each time she pulls on her boots; repeating her *motivating motto* each time she hears the ding of the bell; and thinking of her positive "C" *emotions* each time she passes the letter "C" in the arena.

Concentration cues are a part of a well-known technique called *classical conditioning*. Perhaps the most famous example is the story of noted Russian physiologist Ivan Pavlov and his study of digestion in dogs. He observed that dogs learned to salivate at the ding of a bell when it was rung at the same time as food was presented. In time, he experimented with removing the food and found that his dogs still salivated when the bell was rung even though food wasn't present. He had proved that the dogs had become *conditioned* to think of the food each time they heard the bell.

As a rider you work in much the same way. For example, when you sing your *motivating song* every time you hear the bell in dressage, you'll soon become automatically conditioned to sing it each time you hear the bell (without having to remind yourself to do it). The good news is that when you no longer need to remember to sing your song (because you do it automatically), you can open this book and find another tool to add to

Practice makes perfect even when the practice is mental.

your list. The more tools that become automatic, the more tools you'll be able to remember.

4 Link Your Mental Tools Together—You can remember your Top Three mental tools, but only having to remember two would be even easier. Make this happen by linking at least two of your favorites together. For example, a rider writes the word STAR on a piece of paper (her *cue word*), then just before entering the show arena she crunches it up and shoves it into her boot (her *stress-stopper*). While it might pinch a bit, the sensation reminds her that something's in her boot. What's in her boot? A piece of paper. What's on the paper? STAR. What does STAR stand for? <u>S</u>it <u>T</u>all <u>A</u>nd <u>R</u>elease.

In this example she links two of her Top Three together (her *cue word* and her *stress-stopper*). Let's say her third favorite is *motivating music*. Now she only needs to remember to sing, while using STAR—her *cue word/stress-stopper* pair. The good news is that she only has two things to remember now. She can open this book again and find a new *third* tool to add to her list. The more you're able to link your favorites together, the more tools you'll be able to remember.

5 Build Your Brand—The world's best companies know that creating a strong and recognizable brand can lead to great success: Businesses like Red Bull®, Starbucks®, and Coca Cola® have been doing it for years. You can do the same thing, but instead of building a strong *business* brand, you build a strong *rider* brand. To do this, you link all three of your favorites together and come up with a meaningful *logo* that defines your *brand*.

As an example let's imagine a rider building the brand *SUPER* by link-ing (1) the *cue word* (SUPER—<u>S</u>ucceed <u>U</u>nder <u>P</u>ressure <u>E</u>very <u>R</u>ide) to (2) a *stress-stopper* (wearing a *Superman* T-shirt under her show clothes), to (3) *motivating music* (the song "Superman" by R.E.M.), and to (4) a *motivating motto* ("You're my superman not my minivan.") She could then embroider

a Superman "S" on her saddle pad (as her brand's *logo*) knowing that each time she sees it she'll be reminded of how her *cue word*, *stress-stopper*, *motivating song*, and *motivating motto* are all linked together. In effect, she'll have built her brand and that brand will be *SUPER*.

Another example of a brand is *LUCKY:* Link (1) the *cue word* (LUCKY—<u>L</u>ook <u>U</u>p, <u>C</u>luck, <u>K</u>ick, <u>Y</u>ell) to (2) the *stress-stopper* (rubbing a horseshoe for good *luck)* and to (3) the *motivating music* ("Lucky" by Jason Mraz). You could then embroider a horseshoe logo on your saddle pad as a reminder to always live your "lucky brand."

6 Pay It Forward—Believe it or not, you will forget up to 80 percent of everything you experience every single day. If you fly to another city to look at a horse, by the end of the day you'll probably forget the flight number, the airline's phone number, the pilot's name, and the street name leading to the stable. You experience so many things in the span of a normal day that you just can't possibly process all of them to long-term memory.

There is some good news, however. Even though you may forget up to 80 percent, you will remember up to 90 percent of everything you teach (if you *teach* it, you can *remember* it). For example, a jumper who always forgot her jump courses discovered that she remembered them better if she first taught them to someone—and that someone was her horse! Before riding her course she would say to her horse, "Okay, remember the distance from Fence 1 to 2 is a long four-stride so we've got to get motivated early, and don't forget to balance the landing after Fence 2 because we have a tight rollback over to 3, and from there we've got a short two-stride to the bounce." Ever since she started teaching her courses to her horse she no longer forgets them because she knows that if she teaches it, she'll remember it.

With this in mind, take your Top Three and teach them to someone else. Tell a nervous rider that singing a *motivating song* can make her feel better, and when she feels better she'll be able to ride better. Not only will you have *paid it forward* by helping someone, you'll have also helped yourself by making your Top Three more memorable.

Pressure Proof Plan **Making It Work**

List your top three mental tools:

(1) _____

(2) _____

(3) _____

Write down your *concentration cue:*

_____

_____

_____

Write down your *brand,* including a logo:

_____

_____

PRESSURE PROOF PROJECT

Final Checklist

1 Recall one of your best rides as vividly as you can, remembering what you were thinking, feeling, and experiencing at the time. Then place an X over the number from 1 to 5 for each of the items below that best describes your experience at that time.

2 Recall one of your worst rides ever then similarly place an O over the numbers from 1 to 5 that describe your response.

Felt extremely confident	**1**	**2**	**3**	**4**	**5**	Had no confidence
Felt in complete control	**1**	**2**	**3**	**4**	**5**	Had no control at all
Brain babble was positive	**1**	**2**	**3**	**4**	**5**	Brain babble was negative
Felt extremely focused	**1**	**2**	**3**	**4**	**5**	Felt extremely unfocused
Felt effortless	**1**	**2**	**3**	**4**	**5**	Used a lot of effort
Focused on goals	**1**	**2**	**3**	**4**	**5**	Didn't focus on goals
Felt "in the zone"	**1**	**2**	**3**	**4**	**5**	Felt that nothing went right
Felt strong self-belief	**1**	**2**	**3**	**4**	**5**	Felt a lot of doubt
Stayed focused on self	**1**	**2**	**3**	**4**	**5**	Focused on others
Stayed focus on present	**1**	**2**	**3**	**4**	**5**	Focused on future outcome
Focused on mental image of ride	**1**	**2**	**3**	**4**	**5**	Forgot mental image of ride
Felt well prepared	**1**	**2**	**3**	**4**	**5**	Felt nervous with show jitters
Gave 100 percent	**1**	**2**	**3**	**4**	**5**	Gave less than 100 percent

Rate Your Response

Look at your responses on p. 238, and find the two that have the greatest discrepancy between your best and worst rides. This will indicate the area of mental training that you probably need to focus on the most. Read the chapters in this book covering your two weakest areas, and begin there, using the exercises described in those chapters to become more *Pressure Proof*.

10

Don't Ever Give Up:
Laugh, Learn, and Love

*Your horse doesn't care how much you know
until he knows how much you care.*

Horses Are Unpredictable

The only thing predictable about horses is that they're unpredictable. Our sport is special because of our relationship with horses; you never see a tennis player hugging his racket, or a skier taking his skis for a walk. At the same time, however, you never see a skier having to yell at his ski because it spooked at the snow! Horses are 1,000-pound athletes full of muscle and power, yet they still find a reason to shy at a butterfly.

So what can you do when you've done everything right and something still goes wrong? What can you do when you've sung your songs, rehearsed your ride, and repeated your motto and cue words—all to no avail? The answer is perhaps one of the most difficult things for us to see through—yet perhaps made up of the most important three words in this entire book: *Laugh. Learn. Love.*

**Fall seven times—
get up eight.**

Pressure Proof **Your Future**

1 Laugh

You don't just laugh because you're happy, you're happy because you laugh!

It can be frustrating when you've done everything right and things still go wrong; it's a normal reaction after making an effort but finding it wasn't enough. The main purpose of laughter during adversity is to physically and mentally disrupt the flow of negative emotions. Self-generated laughter in response to frustration or disappointment is called *strategic* or *cathartic* laughter. In times of challenge, it's understandable to feel these negative emotions, but you must do everything you can to disrupt them because they force you to focus on the *problem*, not the *solution*. When it comes to overcoming negative emotions, laughter really is good medicine.

In addition to disrupting the flow of frustration or disappointment, *strategic* laughter also reminds you to laugh at your difficulties right after they happen rather than years later like many people do. In the end, laughing creates happiness and happiness creates the confidence, persistence, optimism, and self-belief. Always attempt to laugh at a situation rather than cry: When your grey horse rolls in the mud you can weep and grit your teeth, or you can take a deep breath, let out a little giggle and say, "Well, I always wanted a Paint."

> **Success in riding is like riding a bike. Never give up. To stay balanced you have to keep moving.**

Laughing Benefits

There are many benefits to be gained from laughter. It:

- Increases the release of endorphin—your body's "stress-reliever" and "feel-good" hormone, which leads to improved focus, mood, self-esteem, and image.

- Decreases the release of the stress hormones dopamine and epinephrine, which can help you avoid feelings of fear, stress, anger, nervousness, or frustration.

- Increases the antibodies in your body that strengthen your immune system. Some studies show that having a positive attitude can extend your life by as much as seven years.

Laughing is easy: It takes 43 muscles to frown but only 17 to smile.

Success may lead to happiness, but happiness also leads to success.

- Increases the flow of oxygen-rich blood to your brain and muscles so that you can move and think more effectively.

- Improves success rates: You're up to three times more likely to achieve success when feeling happy than when feeling sad or tense.

Even though it may not sound like it, *strategic laughter* might just be the single hardest thing suggested in this book. In a sport where hard work is rewarded, it's unusual to think that the hardest thing to do is laugh and stay in a good mood. Up until now frustration and disappointment haven't been a laughing matter, but perhaps, starting today, you should make them one!

2 Learn

Disrupting the flow of frustration and disappointment with a little laughter is important, but after doing so you have another equally important job to do: When you can understand what caused the negative emotions in the first place, you can lessen the chance of them reoccurring in the future.

I'm so far behind I feel like I'm in front!

This is where *learning* comes in. Imagine a horse that is supposed to begin his dressage test at the trot but he's so fresh, he canters into the arena, bucks around for four minutes, and then exits at a canter. It would be completely understandable for the rider to get mad, frustrated, and disappointed, but would it help?

Instead of becoming upset or angry, you could tell your trainer that your horse acted strangely. (She entered at a canter, did wheelies for four minutes, and then ran right out!) The trainer agrees it's unusual so

"We're supposed to enter at a TROT!"

he removes the saddle, palpates the spine, and immediately finds a sensitive area. He then thanks you for bringing it to his attention and calls the chiropractor to take care of it (thereby lessening the chance of it happening again). In this example, *laughter* disrupted the flow of frustration and *learning* helped you understand why it happened in the first place—and what can be done to avoid having it happen in the future.

Missed Opportunity vs. Learning Opportunity

You have the choice of considering disappointment as either a *missed opportunity* or a *learning opportunity*. While these may sound quite similar,

they're actually very different. A learning opportunity is often "disguised" as a missed opportunity or mistake; you just need to be able to see through the disguise and learn from it. In this way, a missed opportunity is what allows you to learn and grow. Many trainers refer to this as "learning the most from our worst lessons." When you can see beyond the disappointment, you can learn from it and improve as a result. Falling is a perfect example. You can feel bad about the fall and just hope no one saw it (no learning), or you can figure out what caused you to fall (learning), so that you can stay in the saddle longer next time.

Learning from Each Other

Most of the time young riders learn from adults (their parents, teachers, trainers, and coaches) but it's also possible for adults to learn from younger riders because they often possess traits that adults can lose over time. These include:

When one teaches— two learn.

- **Laughter** —Children can laugh up to 400 times a day while the average adult laughs only about 17 times a day. It seems that many adults forget how to laugh as they get older. Many also tend to postpone happiness when they pursue goals that cause them to forget to love the *journey* as much as the *destination*.

- **Creativity**—Young riders tend to be very creative. One such rider proved it by writing a message in her calendar saying URGR8 and then set the calendar to deliver the message to herself in the middle of a horse show. (And her *motivating music* was the ring-tone that announced its arrival!) Another proved that, "There's an app for that," by using the smart-phone application Songify to make her very own *motivating music* instead of listening to the music of others.

- **Self-Belief**—Ask a young rider what she's thinking while jumping a 3-foot triple bar and the response is often something like, "I was thinking how nice the purple on the jump matches my saddle pad and how I need to get polo wraps to match it!" Ask the same question of many adults and the answer is often, "I was thinking I'd better not get hurt because I've got to pick the kids up at dance class in an hour!" As we get older, our

Make Believe

A young rider was drawing a picture and when asked what she was coloring, she said, "A picture of God." When her teacher said, "Well we don't really know what God looks like," the youngster thought about it for a second then responded, "Well, you will in a minute." Youngsters just seem to have this natural sense of *self-belief*, the knowledge that what they're doing is easy, correct, and valuable.

daily responsibilities might begin to take a toll on us. Always remember that one of your greatest responsibilities is to have fun and believe in yourself.

- **Focus**—Often blamed for having a short attention span, children actually have the ability to absorb themselves completely and entirely on a task. Just imagine locking an adult in a child's room full of nothing but dolls and teapots. See how long this tea party lasts! As adults we often replace some of our focus and attention with things like worry, fear, and the desire to always know exactly why we're doing what we're doing (remember, *overanalysis leads to paralysis*).

You may not stop laughing because you grow old. You might grow old because you stop laughing.

Youngsters love to test and stretch themselves; that's why we often find children on the top of high ladders, strolling down the middle of the road without a care, or pulling a dog's tail. Between the ages of two and twenty-two we go through many changes and these changes, can cause some of us to lose our *laughter, creativity, self-belief,* and *focus*: we begin to laugh less, worry more, and become preoccupied with being safe and secure. Adults often spend a great deal of time telling children when *not* to laugh (in the car or at the dinner table, for example), but perhaps what we really need is for our children to tell us when *to* laugh (like in the car or at the dinner table)!

3 **Love**

Every one of us started riding for the same reason: pure love of the horse. It was this love that made us want to get out of bed early each morning or rush home from work each afternoon to spend every possible moment

**Riders don't
need big heads,
only big hearts.**

"Can I have the pink one instead of the blue one?"

No __me__—only __we__.

with one. Back then, it wasn't about results or ribbons, podiums or placing, it was all about the horse. When we allow things like frustration, doubt, and anger to enter our minds, we momentarily forget why we became riders in the first place and why we love it so much.

In addition to *laughter, creativity, self-belief* and *focus*, youngsters also have a wonderful ability to love. This love of the horse is what separates our sport from all others and is what makes it so special. A four-year-old girl rode in her first-ever horse show and won all three classes she entered. Upon being presented the blue ribbon (for the third time that day) she leaned over and asked, "Do you think I can have the pink one instead? It's my horse's favorite color." To this youngster, riding wasn't about winning or losing (or even the color of the ribbon), it was something much more. It was about spending time with the one thing in her life that made her the happiest.

So, when you've done everything right but it still goes wrong, always remember to *laugh, learn,* and above all, *love.*

A Final Word

Do what you love. Love what you do.

A riding instructor filled a tack bucket to the top with sponges and asked her students if it was full. They all said, "Yes." She then took a box of pebbles and poured them into the bucket, filling in the spaces between the sponges. She then asked again if the bucket was full. Feeling a little silly that they'd been tricked, they all agreed that it was. The trainer then poured sand into the bucket so that it filled all the spaces between the pebbles. Once again, she asked if the bucket was full. By this time her students had caught on to her tricks so they replied, "Yes, it's now definitely full." She then took a bottle of water and poured the entire thing into the bucket, filling the spaces between all the sand. "Now," she said, "the bucket is full."

The *bucket* in this story represents your riding life. The *sponges* and *pebbles* are the positive emotions like confidence, focus, initiative, resiliency, optimism, commitment, self-respect, self-belief, and self-esteem that allow you to achieve joy, passion, and success. The *sand* and *water* represent all the negative emotions like stress, denial, indecision, withdrawal, anger, frustration, and fear of failure that typically interfere with your ability to achieve joy, passion, and success.

If you live your riding life in such a way that you put the negative sand and water in your bucket first, there won't be any room left for the positive pebbles and sponges. If you spend all your time and energy feeling disappointed after making mistakes; being upset after forgetting your test or course; feeling uncertain after slow starts; or being intimidated because you compare yourself to others, then there won't any room left in your bucket for the things that really make riding the amazingly special sport that it is.

Make a choice to take a chance and make a change!

When it comes to your riding, always remember to fill your bucket with the *sponges* and *stones* of optimism and self-confidence instead of the *sand* and *water* of pessimism and self-criticism. Become the mentally strong and confident rider who always *gets up* instead of *giving up*, who's never satisfied until she goes from *ordinary* to *extraordinary*—the rider who changes from *pressure packed* to *Pressure Proof*.

If you believe it,
you can achieve it.

More Equestrian Sport Psychology Resources from **Daniel Stewart**

Visit my website www.stewartclinics.com **to find:**

- Free downloads of the Pressure Proof Projects in this book.

- Equestrian Sport Psychology CDs available for purchase.

- My tour schedule and information on how to host a Pressure Proof mounted clinic or seminar.

- A chance to sign up for my one-on-one online Sport Psychology Sessions and get started in my Coaching Certification Program.

Index

Eating habits, 218–219
Effort, vs. luck, 58
Emotions
    in goal-setting, 170, 172, 179, 184
    mental toughness and, 52–53
    negative. *see* Destructive emotions
    positive, benefits of, 41. *see also* Positive mental traits
    riding rehearsals and, 147
    types of, 27–28
    visualization and, 145
Encoding, of memories, 228, 229–231
Energizing techniques, 212, 215–216
Ethics, 176, 201
Eustress, vs. distress, 193
Excellence, vs. perfectionism, 79
Excuses, 28, 31, 32, 34, 201
Expectations, 83–84, 96, 195
External focus, 48–49
External incentives, 50–51

Failure, fear of, 75–80, 98, 132, 180–181, 195
"Fake it until you make it," 125, 199
Falling, fear of, 205–206
Fear-driven mindset, 10–11, 51, 82
Feel it to Fix it, 16
Feeler rider type, 12
Fight or flight instinct, 213
Flow states, 64, 66
Focus
    brain structures and, 153–159
    changing, 86, 108
    in children, 248
    on future, 60–61, 76, 85, 172, 186, 194
    goals and, 65, 173
    loss of, 49. *see also* Distractions
    on past, 110, 163, 194
    as positive mental trait, 46–49

on present. *see* Present-moment mindset
    in schooling mindset, 59
    on solutions, 53–55
    targeting and, 207–209
    test of, 164
    types of, 93–94
Future-focused mindset, 60–61, 76, 85, 172, 186, 194

Goal posters, 182–183
Goals
    avoidance of, 180–182
    benefits of, 169–170, 185
    focus on, 65
    kinds of, 5, 170–173
    ladders of, 178–180, 183, 184, 187–188
    legacy and, 185–187
    modifying, 177–178, 186
    motivation for achieving, 182–185
    in overcoming fear of failure, 79
    rating exercise, 188–189
    vs. rewards, 172
    setting of, 173–176
    writing of, 176–180, 182–183
Gratitude, 44–46

Habits, 19, 32, 227–228. *See also* Rituals/routines
Heart rate, stress and, 213–214
Honey do/Honey don't lists, 81, 226–227
Horses. *See also* Rider/horse relationships
    stress in, 195
    unpredictability of, 241
Humor, 52, 63, 84, 136–137, 158–159, 242–244, 247
Hydration, 218–219

"I," 17, 113, 125, 137
"I don't know" mindset, 54, 121–122

Imagery. *See* Mental imagery
Impermanence, law of, 194
Imprinting, 204
"In the zone," 62–66
Inaction, vs. action, 31
Incompetence, 92
Individual Zone of Optimal Functioning (IZOF), 61–62, 63
Inflections, negative, 123
Injury, fear of, 80, 205–206
Internal concentration, 48–49
Internal drives, 49–50
Intimidation, 97–99

Journals, for goal-setting, 178, 184
Judging and judges, fear of, 76–77, 108

Language mediators, 230
Laughter. *See* Humor
Leading questions, 121–124
Learning
    from mistakes, 85–86
    opportunities for, 245–246
    pressure-proofing role, 245–248
    role of failure in, 77–78
    schooling mindset and, 56–59
    from stress, 123
    teaching and, 236–237, 246
Legacy goals, 185–187
Limitations, 33, 78
Logos, 235–236
Long-term goals, 170–171, 174, 179, 182, 183, 184
Long-term memory, 229
Love, 248–250
Luck, vs. effort, 58
Lucky Seven Routine, 219–221

Mechanical behaviors, 153–159, 232, 234
Memory
    overview, 228–229
    in desensitization, 205

Success
    fear of, 76, 181
    as mental skill, 4–8
    motivation for, 11, 51
    role of failure in, 77–78
    soundtrack for, 165

Talking out loud. *See*
    Verbalization
Target dates, for goals, 175, 179
Targeting, 207–209
Teaching, learning and, 236–237,
    246
Technical goals, 170, 172, 179
Telescopic thinking, 83–84
Tension, 59. *See also* Stress
Thought stopping/replacement,
    98, 118–120
Time
    future-focused mindset, 60–
        61, 76, 85, 172, 186, 194

management techniques,
    226–228
past-focused mindset, 110,
    163, 194
present-focused. *see* Present-
    moment mindset
required, for learning mental
    skills, 225–226
in riding rehearsals, 147
sense of, 66
as stressor, 72
target dates, for goals, 175,
    179
"Touchable" items, 157, 198
Toughness training, 41, 199–203
Toxic talk. *See* Negative self-talk
Trainers, role of, 19. *See also*
    Schooling
Trash talking, 126–127, 202
Triggers, 91, 201–202
Trust, in skills, 55–59

Unconscious mind, 92, 105–106,
    111
Universal emotions, 28

Verbalization, 108, 111, 113, 114,
    132
Video analysis, 144
Visualization. *See* Mental imagery

"We," 17, 125, 137
Weaknesses, 13–16, 32–33, 110
Win, vs. winning attitudes, 185
Word substitution, 112–115
Working memory, 229
Writing, uses of, 109, 146, 176–
    180, 184, 186, 231

"Yes, but" response, 44, 46
Young riders, 18–21, 247–248

Zone, riding in, 61–66